GTO POKER GEMS

12 insights from the solver that every player should use

If you are reading this book in black & white, you may notice that some images are difficult to see fully. So we've compiled full-color versions of every image to make your life easier. Download them for free today.

WWW.GTOGEMS.COM/GRAB

GTO GEMS

12 Insights From The Solver That Every Player Should Use

BOOK ISBN INFORMATION:

9798418686299

BOOK WEBSITE:

www.redchippoker.com/gtogems

CONTACT:

Feel free to reach out to me directly to discuss permission to reproduce selections from this book, business development, coaching, collaboration, or future projects.

My best email address is james@splitsuit.com

PREFACE

The application of game theory optimal (GTO) concepts to poker has continued to grow in popularity over the years. You can see it clearly by looking at the Google Trends output for the term:

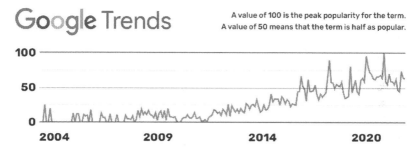

Google Trends

A value of 100 is the peak popularity for the term. A value of 50 means that the term is half as popular.

There is no reason to believe this trend will cease any time soon, and it explains why you have already seen a dramatic increase in available solvers, GTO ranges, videos on the topic, and so on.

But the concept of GTO poker has also created considerable confusion and division among players. Some players claim to play a GTO strategy, while others scoff at the idea of playing anything other than 100% exploitative. Others take a middling approach by implementing a hybrid of both GTO and exploitative strategies.

So who is correct? What role does GTO really play in today's games? What role should GTO play in your overall strategy?

This book aims to answer these kinds of questions while giving you applicable advice from the GTO solvers.

The goal is not to overload you with complex solver output that is impossible to understand, let alone implement. The goal is to distill the gems into big-picture ideas that you can actually use (no randomizer needed!).

If you are newer to GTO, be sure to take your time through the early chapters, since they lay the foundation for the latter ideas. You do not need a GTO solver to get complete value from this book, but a solver can help you explore these concepts further in both simplified and complex examples.

The solver we used for the models in this book is called GTO+ (made by the same team that created Flopzilla Pro). We offer a special bundle with a lifetime license to GTO+, along with a complete course on utilizing this solver, plus every save file so you can instantly fire up the same game trees.

Pick up your copy today by going to www.gtogems.com/bundle

Regardless of the GTO solver you use, and even if you opt not to use one at this time, you can lean on the exploration in this book to make sense of key strategic ideas.

So let us grab our shovels and together start digging for those gems!

THE GTO RANGES APP

Your preflop ranges are the foundation of your poker strategy.

Simply put, playing the proper number and types of hands from the correct positions will set you up for success. Playing too loose preflop, or too tight, will make postflop play more difficult.

This is why we created *The GTO Ranges App*. Now all of your preflop ranges are in your pocket at all times. A few taps in the app and you see exactly what you should be playing, how you should be playing it, and from which positions.

WWW.GTOGEMS.COM/APP

On top of including our GTO preflop ranges in the app, we also added our popular exploitative ranges from both CORE and PRO.

This means you get a wide variety of battle-tested ranges meant for both soft games (like micro limits online and $1/$2 live cash games) and tougher games where more GTO-oriented ranges are a must.

Download the complete app today to get:

- 6-max cash game ranges

- Live cash game ranges

- Tournament ranges

- Access to all future solves & ranges

- Favoriting (for quick access to ranges you regularly use)

- Offline access

And as a special bonus for picking up this book, you can immediately **save $10 every year** for the app when you grab an annual plan and use the code **GEMS** today.

Just visit www.gtogems.com/app, enter the code GEMS at checkout, then download and begin using the app.

Keep your preflop ranges in your pocket with *The GTO Ranges App* from Red Chip Poker.

TABLE OF CONTENTS

GTO+ FILES

All of the GTO solver models in this book were created and analyzed using the GTO+ software. To make your life easier, and to allow you to follow along with the analysis in this book, we made all of the save files/ game trees available to you for free.

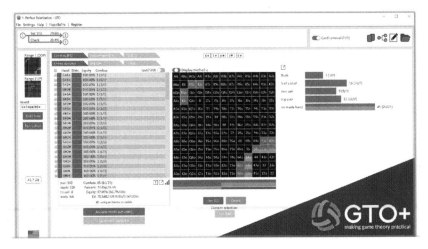

Grab all of them by visiting www.gtogems.com/models

Simply save the files to a folder on your computer and within GTO+ go to File > Open and navigate to the aforementioned folder. These trees are already created and crunched, so you can begin exploring the ranges and output immediately.

If you have any questions, please be sure to join our Discord server and post in the GTO Gems channel at www.gtogems.com/discord

THERE IS A SOLUTION TO POKER

From the earliest days of poker, there were players who recognized that the game had an element of skill. But why did some players seem to win so consistently? Were they simply the luckiest players on the planet?

We can now prove beyond reasonable doubt that, although poker has elements of short-term luck, in the long-term it is a game of pure skill. Over a sufficiently large sample of hands, a skilled poker player will always win when playing against weaker opposition.

Like many other games of skill, poker has an optimal solution. This means that there are objectively right and wrong answers to the tough decisions we face at the poker tables.

WHAT IS AN *OPTIMAL SOLUTION*?

When poker players talk about an "optimal solution," they mean something very specific. They are referring to a mathematically-perfect game theory optimal (GTO) solution.

GAME THEORY OPTIMAL (GTO)

Game theory is a branch of mathematics that deals with calculating strategies for competitive situations (such as playing poker and other strategy games). If a poker decision is game theory optimal, it means it is mathematically the best possible decision when facing a perfect opponent.

When a poker player follows a perfect GTO strategy, it is impossible for them to be beaten. The absolute worst-case scenario is that they will break even when facing an advanced opponent who is also using a GTO strategy. Against unskilled opposition, a perfect GTO strategy will make significant profits.

Sounds good, right? We are guaranteed to either win or tie against everyone we play against. So how exactly do we get started with playing perfect GTO poker?

THE GTO SOLUTION TO POKER

Let us start with the bad news. The complete GTO solution to popular poker variants like NLHE and PLO is not known at this time. Further, no such solution is anticipated in the foreseeable future. The number of different possible actions, boards, hands, and bet sizes in these variants is so vast that it would take an unrealistic amount of time to generate a complete GTO solution.

Put another way, the game tree (all possible actions, boards, hands and bet sizings) is too large to allow a full GTO solution to be generated, even using powerful modern computers.

GAME TREE

A game tree is a diagram containing all the possible game states for a certain game. In poker, the game tree represents all the possible actions, boards, hands, and bet sizes that are possible across the entire game. Game trees in complex games like poker or chess can become enormous.

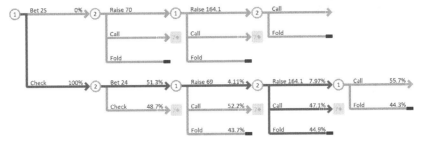

A GTO+ GAME TREE FOR A SINGLE STREET WITH A SINGLE BET SIZING OPTION

The good news is that we can still make extremely good estimates of what GTO poker looks like by making use of a *simplified* game tree.

Imagine a heads-up (HU) poker game where players have limited options. For example, perhaps they are only allowed to bet half-pot, check, or call at every decision point. The GTO solution to such a game is now simple enough that any amateur with a basic laptop can calculate the full solution using GTO poker software.

SOLVERS: GTO POKER SOFTWARE

There is now commercially-available software that provides the game theory optimal solution for a given game tree. These tools are referred to as solvers or GTO solvers by the poker community.

GTO SOLVER

In poker circles, the term solver refers to computer software that can calculate GTO poker solutions for a given game tree. They are commercially available to anyone and will run on most modern systems.

Note that solvers do not provide a full GTO solution to poker as we have discussed above. They provide a GTO solution for a given (but simplified) game tree. Almost every GTO solver will have an interface that allows the user to construct and configure their preferred game tree.

You will not need a GTO solver in order to make use of this book. Our objective is to teach you valuable GTO poker concepts, without the need for you to run complex solver analysis.

However, you may prefer to purchase a commercial solver anyway if you are looking for a deeper dive into some of the concepts we discuss.

If you are interested in using the same solver we use for our postflop solves, coupled with a complete training course for using it correctly, please visit www.gtogems.com/solver

WHAT DO GTO SOLUTIONS LOOK LIKE?

There is a great irony behind the quest for the full GTO poker solution.

Imagine for a moment that a futuristic space alien dropped the complete GTO solution to poker onto our desk.

We are in for untold riches, right?

Not exactly.

The first problem we would run into is that our desk would likely collapse under the weight of several trillion pieces of paper. The full GTO solution to poker is huge. (Please do not ask why the futuristic alien is using regular paper and not telepathy.)

Let us say, purely hypothetically, that we convinced our personal assistant to work a ridiculous amount of overtime and collate all of that information into an easy-to-access digital format. This is when we run into our second big problem.

The GTO strategy is so complex that it is virtually impossible to execute correctly.

But in what way is the strategy complex? It is just a case of making the decision to either call, fold, or raise at the right time? In detail, no.

One lesson we learn from simplified game tree solves is that GTO poker makes heavy use of *mixed strategies*.

MIXED STRATEGY

A mixed strategy is one in which a certain poker hand is required to take differing actions at certain frequencies. For example, when facing a bet, GTO poker might require a hand to call 70% of the time and raise 30% of the time.

Note that when a hand instead takes a certain action with 100% frequency (for example, it *always* calls), this is usually referred to as a *pure strategy*.

Rather than simply call or raise, imagine a hand that needs to raise 17.4% of the time, call 37.8% of the time, and fold 44.8% of the time. Imagine that these frequencies change with every hand we are dealt, on every street we play, and against every single bet size we face.

Humans simply do not have the mental capacity to track these types of complex frequencies over tens of thousands of hands. Alas, when we finally uncover the full solution to poker, only machines (or savants) will be able to accurately execute the solution.

THE RELEVANCE OF GTO POKER

If playing GTO poker is something that we can never realistically achieve, we might question why we should bother exploring the world of GTO poker at all.

Put simply, we do not need to play perfect GTO poker in order to win at poker. We just need to have a better understanding of the game than our average opponent.

Exploring GTO concepts can dramatically improve the way we think about poker strategy, as well as allowing us to dominate the majority of our opponents.

An important starting point is to appreciate the following:

The goal of learning GTO poker is not necessarily to play GTO poker.

The goal of learning GTO is mostly to get a better understanding of the mistakes our opponents are making and how we can exploit those mistakes. Exploiting our opponents' mistakes will be more profitable than rigidly adhering to a GTO style of poker.

Why exactly is that the case? We can find the answer by analyzing a well-known game that has an extremely simple game tree. The game is usually known as *Rock, Paper, Scissors.*

GTO VERSUS EXPLOITATIVE: RPS

It is highly likely that you already know how this game works.

But assuming you have been living under a rock (pun slightly intended), let us recap briefly.

Rock, paper, scissors (RPS) is a two-person game in which each player chooses either rock, paper, or scissors without letting their opponent know their selection beforehand.

Once both players reveal their selection, the scoring table is simply:

- Rock beats scissors.

- Scissors beat paper.

- Paper beats rock.

- If both players choose the same item, the result is a tie.

It just so happens that RPS is an example of a solved game.

The game theory optimal strategy for RPS is to choose each option exactly one third of the time. Using this strategy, we will always win exactly one third of our games and tie one third of our games in the long run.

It does not matter how our opponent modifies their strategy. There is absolutely nothing our opponent can do to prevent us from winning exactly one third of our games.

The perfect GTO strategy for RPS ends up with neither player winning in the long run. The end result is a tie.

Poker is similar. When two perfect GTO poker players play heads up, the result is that neither player will make a profit in the long run.

Imagine our RPS opponent was not very experienced and decided to pick "rock" with a 100% frequency. If we continued with our GTO RPS strategy, our long-term results would still be a tie.

DID YOU KNOW?

To use game theory lingo, RPS is referred to as a *strongly-solved* game, since every aspect of the game is understood thoroughly. Specifically, a complete solution to the game is known. This should not come as a big surprise since the game itself is so basic. Poker, on the other hand, is not considered solved. The exception is HU LHE which is considered *weakly solved*.

Is that our best strategic response in this situation?

Ideally, we would switch to choosing "paper" every single round if we knew our opponent would continue to only pick "rock." We would win 100% of our games this way. We would no longer be playing a game theory optimal strategy, but instead would be implementing an *exploitative* strategy.

EXPLOITATIVE

A strategy that is not considered game theory optimal, but is designed to take advantage of the mistakes that our opponent is making. (A "mistake" is any deviation our opponent makes from perfect GTO play). Exploitative play in poker has the potential to win more money than a game theory optimal strategy.

We can similarly make more money in poker by playing exploitatively, rather than using GTO strategies.

Knowledge of GTO poker is extremely valuable because it allows us to recognize when our opponents are making errors. Further, GTO strategies provide a baseline from which we deviate exploitatively.

KEEPING SCORE IN POKER

In RPS, the winner is simply the person who wins the most rounds since every round is valued the same.

This is not true in poker.

A player who wins more hands does not necessarily win the overall game, because different amounts of chips are wagered on each hand.

The profitability of various decisions in poker is measured using *expected value* (EV).

This is a very important GTO poker concept that we will be using throughout this book.

EXPECTED VALUE (EV)

A measurement of how profitable a poker decision is on average, measured in either big blinds or a currency amount (e.g., dollars).

Take note of the following common terms used by poker players.

If you are not completely sure how to use or calculate EV, you can get the formula along with examples here: www.gtogems.com/ev

TERM	MEANING
+EV or "plus EV"	This decision is profitable in the long run.
-EV or "minus EV"	This decision will lose money in the long run.
"Max EV"	This is the most profitable decision that is available.
"This decision is worth 5bb in EV"	We will make 5 big blinds on average over the long run with this decision. (The short-term results will vary based on luck though).

DID YOU KNOW?

Unlike the GTO strategy for RPS, GTO poker does *not* break even against everyone. Although GTO poker breaks even against another perfect GTO opponent, it will generate a positive win-rate against opponents who are making strategic mistakes.

THE GEMS

- While a complete GTO solution may exist for complex games like NLHE and PLO, it will be impossible for a human to accurately implement.

- You do not need to play perfect GTO poker in order to win.

- Exploiting your opponents' mistakes will be more profitable than rigidly sticking to a GTO approach.

- Simple games, like RPS, offer a clear visualization for using versus deviating from a GTO solution.

- A player who wins more hands does not necessarily win the overall game, because different amounts of chips are wagered on each hand.

GEM #2

UNEXPLOITABLE BLUFFING

Even before the days of GTO analysis, the best poker players intuitively understood that there was a limit to how much bluffing they could get away with.

A well-timed bluff can undoubtedly be very lucrative, but if you start bluffing *all* of the time, even the most obtuse of opponents will catch on to the exploitation that is taking place.

Conversely, if we are never bluffing, it becomes too easy for opponents to simply fold strong second-best hands when we bet, recognizing that we almost always have an even stronger holding.

The solution?

Just like *Rock, Paper, Scissors*, we need to mix up our lines.

If we can build our betting *ranges* with a good balance of bluffs and value bets, it makes it much harder for our opponent to exploit us.

> **RANGE**
>
> Short for *a range of possible holdings*. The term refers to all of the hands with which a player might take a specific action. Advanced poker players tend to think in terms of ranges of hands rather than individual hands. For an expanded definition and examples, read this guide: www.gtogems.com/ranges

A bluff is a bet made with a very weak hand that aims to get our opponent to fold. A value bet is a bet made with a strong hand (i.e., a *value* hand) that aims to get called by worse holdings.

A PERFECT BLUFFING STRATEGY

GTO analysis teaches us that there is a perfect balance between the number of bluffs and the number of value hands that we should bet in a given situation. This balance is referred to as the *bluff-to-value ratio* or *bluff:value*.

> ## BLUFF-TO-VALUE RATIO
>
> A bluff-to-value ratio describes the relative number of value hands and bluffs that we have in our range when we bet or raise. E.g., a 1:2 (one-to-two) bluff-to-value ratio means we are bluffing half as often as we are value betting. Alternatively, we might say that one third (~33%) of our range consists of bluffs.

Having the perfect bluff-to-value ratio not only makes it difficult for our opponent to play against us, it actually makes it completely impossible for our opponent to construct a winning counter-strategy. A perfect bluff-to-value ratio is the equivalent of always choosing each option in RPS exactly one third of the time.

But what does the perfect bluff-to-value ratio look like?

To understand this, we need to first lay some important groundwork.

A SIMPLE GTO MODEL

It is common to make some simplifications and assumptions when applying game theory to poker. We will be making use of the following common assumptions when discussing bluff-to-value ratios.

ASSUMPTION 1: WE ARE ANALYZING A RIVER SITUATION

The concept of bluff-to-value ratios applies mainly to river situations. The model we are about to discuss will not apply directly to earlier street scenarios.

We will consider a HU situation where one player (the aggressor) makes a bet against their opponent (the defender) on the river.

ASSUMPTION 2: THE AGGRESSOR HAS A "PERFECTLY POLARIZED" RANGE

The aggressor has a betting range consisting purely of value hands and bluffs; that is, perfectly polarized.

POLARIZED

A polarized range is comprised exclusively of strong value hands and bluffs, with no hand strengths in between.

The value hands can never lose at showdown, and the bluffs can never win at showdown. The aggressor is first to act (out of position) on the river.

ASSUMPTION 3: THE DEFENDER HAS A RANGE OF PURE BLUFF-CATCHERS

None of the hands in the defender's range can ever beat the aggressor's value hands at showdown. However, all of the hands in the defender's range will always win at showdown against the aggressor's bluffs. The defender is last to act (in position) on the river.

The term bluff-catcher refers to a hand that can only win if our opponent is bluffing. In the context of a GTO discussion, a bluff-catcher will also be at least strong enough to beat all of our opponent's bluffs.

DID YOU KNOW?

Attempts have been made to apply the concept of bluff-to-value ratios to earlier streets but such models have a number of problems and inaccuracies. The main issue is that it is difficult to define terms such as bluff or value hand when future community cards can completely change the relative strength of our hand. It is generally easier to assume that the concept of bluff-to-value ratios only applies to river play.

This outlined model, along with all of the assumptions, is sometimes referred to as the *perfect polarization model*. Take a moment to make sure you have a good understanding of the scenario since it will crop up quite frequently in conversations about GTO poker.

Polarized range (value hands and bluffs only).
Value hands always win at showdown.
Bluffs always lose at showdown.

A range of pure bluff-catchers.
Bluff-catchers always beat bluffs.
Bluff-catchers always lose to value hands.

THE PERFECT BLUFFING FREQUENCY

When making use of the perfect polarization model, the perfect bluff to value ratio is entirely dependent on the size of the aggressor's bet.

The easiest way of calculating the perfect bluffing frequency for the aggressor is simply to consider the pot odds that the defender gets when facing a bet.

POT ODDS

Pot odds refers to the price a player gets on a call when facing a bet. This can be expressed as a ratio or as a percentage of the total pot invested. For more: www.gtogems.com/potodds

Take a simple example where the aggressor bets $100 into a $100 pot on the river with a perfectly polarized range.

How often should they be bluffing?

Let us start by calculating the pot odds that the defender is getting.

The defender would be risking $100 to win the $200 pot. They are therefore getting ~33% pot odds on the call (or 2:1, if you prefer ratios).

As the aggressor, we should bluff the same percentage as the pot odds the defender is being offered: ~33% (or one third) of the time. The remaining ~67% (or two thirds) of our betting range should be value hands. If we instead use ratios we can say that our bluff-to-value ratio should be 1:2 (one-to-two), which is simply the pot odds ratio switched around.

It is impossible for our opponent to exploit us if we play this way given the proposed situation.

Of course, knowing the optimal bluffing frequency does not automatically mean we understand how, or why, it works! Let us take a look at that now.

HOW DOES A PERFECT BLUFFING STRATEGY *ACTUALLY* WORK?

Remember in our example that the defender holds a bluff-catcher, which means that they will *only* win if the aggressor is bluffing.

Think for a moment about the following questions: Should the defender call the river with their bluff-catcher? On what factors is the decision dependent?

The answer depends purely on the defender's pot odds.

The defender can call profitably if they expect to win more often than their pot-odds percentage. Let us break it down.

If the aggressor is bluffing more than one third of the time, the defender should always call because it will be +EV (profitable) for them to do so. The aggressor is bluffing too frequently according to game theory.

If the aggressor is bluffing less than one third of the time, the defender should always fold because calling will be -EV (unprofitable). The aggressor is not bluffing frequently enough according to game theory.

If, however, the aggressor bluffs at the perfect frequency, exactly one third of the time, there is nothing that the defender can do to exploit the aggressor. It is only if the aggressor deviates from the optimal bluffing frequency that the defender is able to generate an exploitative counter-strategy, in which the defender either always calls or always folds.

The following table shows the three possible scenarios along with the implications of the defender's EV.

SCENARIO	DEFENDER EV
The aggressor bluffs more than one third of the time with a pot-sized bet.	**Calling is +EV. Folding is 0EV.** The defender can maximize their win-rate by *always calling*.
The aggressor bluffs exactly one third of the time with a pot-sized bet.	**Calling is 0EV. Folding is 0EV.** The defender cannot change their win-rate by adjusting their strategy.
The aggressor bluffs less than one third of the time with a pot-sized bet.	**Calling is -EV. Folding is 0EV.** The defender can maximize their win-rate by *always folding*.

ATTEMPTING TO COUNTER

Let us play devil's advocate for a moment and try to increase the defender's EV by playing around with their strategy. We know that folding more will not help the defender, since the EV of folding will always be zero.

Instead, consider the defender's EV when they call to see if you can increase their profits.

There are two possible outcomes that can occur when the defender calls the river with a bluff-catcher. The following is an example of how we calculate the EV of this simple poker spot.

EV CALCULATION

Scenario 1: The bluff-catcher wins $200 because the aggressor is bluffing. This happens one third of the time and wins $66.66 per hand in the long run.

Scenario 2: The bluff-catcher loses $100 because the aggressor is value betting. This happens two thirds of the time and loses $66.66 per hand in the long run.

TOTAL EV = $66.66 - $66.66 = **$0 EV**

The amount the defender wins when the aggressor is bluffing is perfectly balanced by the amount the defender loses when the aggressor is value betting. We have demonstrated that the expected value of calling the river with a bluff-catcher is exactly $0!

DID YOU KNOW?

No matter what the defender does in the above scenario, their EV will always be zero. Even if the defender always calls, always folds, or mixes up their calling and folding ranges arbitrarily, their EV will always be zero.

We usually express this by saying that the defender is *indifferent* between calling or folding with their bluff-catchers.

This is not to say that the defender's calling frequency is not important. For example, if the defender chooses to fold every single time, this is something that the aggressor can potentially exploit.

OUR FIRST SIMPLE SOLVER MODEL

Many of the discussions in this book are based upon real solver models. We will start by employing the perfect polarization model and running it through a GTO solver.

It is not necessary to run these solves yourself since we will provide all of the required information. However, we have made the GTO+ solver files available for those who are interested in a deeper dive. Grab them by visiting www.gtogems.com/solverfiles

Here are the starting ranges we used in *Solver Model 1: Perfect Polarization*. Note that the ranges are not designed to be *realistic* but rather to represent the perfect polarization model as simply and accurately as possible.

BOARD

AGGRESSOR (OOP)		DEFENDER (IP)

AA	AK	AQ	AJ	AT	A9	A8	A7	A6	A5	A4	A3	A2
AK	KK	KQ	KJ	KT	K9	K8	K7	K6	K5	K4	K3	K2
AQ	KQ	QQ	QJ	QT	Q9	Q8	Q7	Q6	Q5	Q4	Q3	Q2
AJ	KJ	QJ	JJ	JT	J9	J8	J7	J6	J5	J4	J3	J2
AT	KT	QT	JT	TT	T9	T8	T7	T6	T5	T4	T3	T2
A9	K9	Q9	J9	T9	99	98	97	96	95	94	93	92
A8	K8	Q8	J8	T8	98	88	87	86	85	84	83	82
A7	K7	Q7	J7	T7	97	87	77	76	75	74	73	72
A6	K6	Q6	J6	T6	96	86	76	66	65	64	63	62
A5	K5	Q5	J5	T5	95	85	75	65	55	54	53	52
A4	K4	Q4	J4	T4	94	84	74	64	54	44	43	42
A3	K3	Q3	J3	T3	93	83	73	63	53	43	33	32
A2	K2	Q2	J2	T2	92	82	72	62	52	42	32	22

AGGRESSOR (OOP)	DEFENDER (IP)
KQs–KJs, 63s–62s, 54s–52s, KQo–KJo, 63o–62o, 54o–52o	T9s–T7s, T9o–T7o

Note that the aggressor's bluffs here are any 5x hand that does not have a diamond flush by the river. On the other hand, the defender's range always makes a pair of tens which always beats the aggressor's bluffs, but loses to the aggressor's value range.

Here is a breakdown of how the solver is playing the river as the aggressor. If you are unfamiliar with the concept of *combos*, the term combo is used when discussing how many ways a type of hand can be made. For example, there are six possible ways to be dealt a given pocket pair preflop, so there are six combos of each pocket pair.

HAND CATEGORY	# OF COMBOS	% OF BETTING RANGE
Value Betting Range	40	66.67%
Bluffing Range	20	33.33%
Overall Betting Range	60	100%

Notice that the solver is bluffing exactly one third of the time when making a pot-sized river bet.

THE GEMS

- We should bet a mixture of bluffs and value hands on the river. (This is known as betting a polarized range.)

- The larger our river bet sizing, the more frequently we should be bluffing.

- Value bets should account for the larger portion of our range, even when using large sizes.

- The GTO bluffing frequency for the aggressor is the same as the pot odds percentage offered to the defender.

FINAL ADVICE

Avoid getting bogged down with precise bluffing frequencies. Even being *somewhere in the right ballpark* with your bluff-to-value ratio will make you a lot tougher to play against.

PREVENTING THEIR +EV BLUFFS

Do you ever have the feeling you are being run over by an advanced opponent?

As poker players, we inherently understand that there is a limit to the amount of folding we should be doing (unless we hate money). If we fold too much our opponent can take advantage of us by bluffing relentlessly.

On the other hand, we are also probably aware that players who call too much typically end up being big losing players. Folding with some frequency has to be correct, otherwise, it becomes too easy for our opponent to extract value with big hands.

Fortunately, GTO analysis provides us with the perfect middle ground between folding too much and calling like a maniac.

THE PERFECT MIDDLE GROUND

In order to prevent our opponents from being able to bluff profitably, we first need to recall what makes a bluff profitable in the first place.

Begin by answering this question: The aggressor makes a bluff of $100 into a $100 pot on the river. How often does their bluff need to work in order to be profitable?

This is similar to a pot-odds calculation from the previous chapter. We can simply look at what percentage of the total pot is being invested.

The total pot here is $200 (including our opponent's bet). Our opponent is therefore investing $100/$200, or 50% of the total pot.

This value is known as the break-even point or the auto-profit threshold of the bluff.

BREAK-EVEN POINT

Also known as the *auto-profit threshold*, this refers to how often a bluff needs to work in order to be profitable in the long run. If a bluff works more frequently than the break-even point, it will be profitable. If the bluff works less often than the break-even point, it will be an outright losing bet.

Perhaps unsurprisingly, if a bluff works at exactly the same frequency as the break even point it will "break even," or have an EV of 0.

APPLYING THE PREVIOUS MODEL

Let us revisit the perfect polarization model that we used in the previous chapter. The aggressor is using a pot-sized bet, which means that the break-even threshold on their bluff is 50%.

If we fold more frequently than our opponent's auto-profit threshold, they can exploit us by bluffing relentlessly.

If the defender folds more frequently than 50%, the aggressor can bluff profitably with all of their air hands.

If the defender folds less frequently than 50%, the aggressor can remove all bluffs as an exploit.

If the defender folds *exactly* 50% of the time, there is nothing the aggressor can do to exploit the defender.

That 50% defending frequency is the perfect middle ground in our perfect polarization model.

ATTEMPTING TO COUNTER

For a moment, we are going to talk to Fred. Fred refuses to believe that the aggressor's EV cannot be changed. But we can prove this to Fred by exploring the EV of a bluff.

Note that the calculations in this chapter can be confirmed by loading

Solver Model 1: Perfect Polarization. The calculations will be written out to give you an intuitive feel for how EV works, but feel free to skip straight to the results if you find that doing arithmetic will ruin your day.

BLUFFING EV CALCULATION

Scenario 1: Villain folds and the aggressor wins $100. This happens 50% of the time and **wins $50 per hand** in the long run.

Scenario 2: Villain calls and the aggressor loses $100. This happens 50% of the time and **loses $50 per hand** in the long run.

TOTAL EV = $50 - $50 = $0 EV

This calculation demonstrates that a 50% folding frequency is the break-even point of the pot-sized bluff because the EV is 0.

So how about value betting?

VALUE BETTING EV CALCULATION

Scenario 1: The aggressor's value bet gets paid off and wins a total of $200 (the $100 in the pot and the $100 that the defender calls). This happens 50% of the time and **wins $100 per hand** in the long run.

Scenario 2: The defender folds and the aggressor wins the $100 in the middle. This happens 50% of the time and **wins $50 per hand** in the long run.

TOTAL EV = $100 + $50 = $150 EV

Notice that value betting is +EV for the aggressor and nets them $150 per hand in this example. Does this mean that the aggressor is beating the system because they are now generating profit? *No.*

It is *normal* for a value bet to be profitable even when playing GTO poker.

The goal of the defender is not to *prevent* the aggressor from profiting. This would be impossible. The aggressor is in an inherently profitable situation because of their strong value hands.

Rather, the goal of the defender is to prevent the aggressor from making *more* than the maximum amount of profit to which the aggressor is entitled, given the situation.

Provided the defender does not fold less than 50% of the time, the EV of a value bet for the aggressor is capped at $150.

THE EV OF VILLAIN'S RANGE

It is possible for us to calculate the EV not just of individual holdings in the aggressor's range, but rather the EV of their *entire* betting range.

BETTING EV CALCULATION

Scenario 1: The aggressor is value betting, which carries an EV of $150. This happens two thirds of the time and **wins $100 per hand** in the long run.

Scenario 2: The aggressor is bluffing, which carries an EV of $0. This happens one third of the time and **loses $0 per hand** in the long run.

TOTAL EV = $100 - $0 = $100 EV

Here is the interesting part. What happens if the aggressor modifies their strategy and removes all of the bluffs, making their betting range 100% value hands?

ZERO BLUFFING EV CALCULATION

Scenario 1 (the only scenario): The aggressor is value betting, which carries an EV of $150 (as previously calculated). This happens 100% of the time and **wins $150 per hand** in the long run.

TOTAL EV = $150 EV

Okay, what?!? Did we just break GTO?

Did we just manage to somehow increase the EV of the aggressor's betting range after we promised you that it was impossible to do so?

Avoid panicking just yet. Let us explain.

It is true that the EV of the betting range itself just increased. However, the EV of the *overall* strategy for the aggressor likely just got worse. After all, the aggressor must be checking a lot more and betting less frequently now.

Consider a player, Nate, who only plays AA in NLHE. Nate's EV when he actually enters a pot is amazing since his range is exclusively AA. However, is Nate making more money than a seasoned professional? Almost certainly not, since nitty Nate is playing too tight of a range preflop, and the blinds are slowly eating him alive.

What is the lesson? GTO poker is not just about maximizing the EV of an *individual* range. GTO poker is about maximizing our EV across our *entire strategy*. This, in turn, involves continuing with as many hands as mathematically possible, provided they are not -EV.

This brings us to another elephant in the room that must be addressed. In our previous scenario, the aggressor is now firing with an unbalanced bluff-to-value ratio.

Let us look at the adjusted EV of the aggressor if the defender makes the correct exploitative adjustment of folding at 100% frequency.

BETTING VS. ZERO DEFENSE EV CALCULATION

Scenario 1 (the only scenario): The defender folds and the aggressor wins $100. This happens 100% of the time and wins $100 per hand in the long run.

TOTAL EV = $100 EV

That number should look familiar. It is the original EV that the aggressor had for their range when following a balanced strategy. The overall EV of the aggressor's strategy just got worse though, since they are firing less often after removing all of their bluffs.

Previously, the aggressor's bluffs were technically netting them $100 on average (as part of that balanced betting range), whereas now, the aggressor is presumably losing with 100% frequency at showdown when the river gets checked through.

Things could be a lot worse though.

Let us see what happens if the aggressor shifts to a range of 100% bluffs against the optimal defender.

BLUFFING ENTIRE RANGE EV CALCULATION

Scenario: The aggressor is bluffing, which carries an EV of $0 since they win the $100 pot when the defender folds 50% of the time, and they lose $100 when the defender calls and wins 50% of the time. This strategy **wins $0 per hand** in the long run.

TOTAL EV = $0 EV

That does not look great for the aggressor.

And that assumes the defender is closing their eyes and continuing to defend exactly 50% of the time. If the defender is playing well, they will now call 100% of the time.

BLUFFING VS. 100% DEFENSE EV CALCULATION

Scenario: The defender calls and the aggressor loses their $100 bet. This happens 100% of the time and **loses $100 per hand** in the long run.

TOTAL EV = -$100 EV

If there is an official poker definition of *hemorrhaging money*, this is probably it.

As we discussed earlier, the EV of the range does not necessarily tell us the EV of the entire strategy. The value hands (which are presumably now checking) will have a positive expected value at showdown since they will always win against the defender's bluff-catchers. However, those same value hands will not be making as much as they could be if played correctly.

Using *Solver Model 1: Perfect Polarization* we are able to confirm our assumptions.

The defender has 36 different possible hands and folds exactly 18 (50%) of them.

We can also confirm that the EV of bluffing is $0, the EV of value betting is $150, and the EV of the overall betting range is $100.

CONCLUSIONS FOR THE DEFENDER

In the perfect polarization model, the defender should *call at a frequency that makes the aggressor's bluffs 0EV.*

While it is true that the defender could potentially lower the EV of the aggressor's value bets by folding more often, the defender would then open themselves up to counter exploitation since the aggressor could start bluffing extremely aggressively.

It is also true that the defender can make the EV of the aggressor's bluffs less than zero by calling more often, but the defender would again open the door to counter-exploitation, since the aggressor could then remove all of their -EV bluffs as an exploit.

It should hopefully be clearer why the GTO solution for the defender is folding exactly 50% is in our model.

THE GEMS

- There is a perfect middle ground between how often we fold and how often we continue against our opponent's bets.

- The larger our opponent's bet sizing, the more often we should fold.

- We can calculate the break-even point of our opponent's bluff by looking at the percentage of the total pot they are investing.

- We should defend at a frequency that makes our opponent's bluffs 0EV (assuming the perfect polarization model).

FINAL ADVICE

Avoid getting bogged down with precise defense frequencies. Even being *somewhere in the right ballpark* with how often to defend will make you a *lot* tougher to play against.

ALWAYS MAXIMIZE EV

It is not uncommon to hear poker players talk about a type of poker hand known as a *loss leader*. It is a theoretical concept that has ultimately been disproved by the use of poker solvers.

A loss leader is a hand that is deliberately played at a lower EV than it is worth. The idea is that, by sacrificing EV with certain hands, we can boost the EV of other hands within our range.

EVIDENCE WITHIN SOLVER MODELS

Let us examine some of the hands from the aggressor's betting range in *Solver Model 1: Perfect Polarization* along with their expected values.

BOARD

HAND	STRATEGY	BET EV	CHECK EV
KQ (top pair)	Always Bet	$150	$100
5d4d (flush)	Always Bet	$150	$100
53o (bluff)	Bet: 44.4% Check: 55.6%	$0	$0
54o (bluff)	Bet: 44.4% Check: 55.6%	$0	$0

Upon further examination, it looks like all of the value hands bet 100%

of the time, while all of the air hands are played as mixed strategies.

Take a moment to think about the numbers in the previous table. Can they teach us anything about GTO play?

LESSON 1: THE SOLVER ALWAYS MAXIMIZES EV

If the theory behind loss leaders were true, we might expect to see the solver sometimes checking the river with a value hand in the above model, despite the calculated EV of a check being $50 *lower* than that of betting.

However, regardless of how complex a solver model is, we *never* see a solver playing a hand at an EV lower than its potential maximum.

We find that the way we maximize the EV of our overall strategy is by playing every individual hand at its maximum EV. We cannot boost the EV of our overall strategy by deliberately lowering the EV of specific hands.

Solvers have essentially disproved the concept of loss leaders.

LESSON 2: MIXED STRATEGIES ARE MANDATORY

Looking at the air hands in the previous table, we notice that the solver is employing a mixed strategy. Let us take a moment to reflect on why this is the case.

In our perfect polarization model, the aggressor reaches the river with 45 air combos and 40 value combos. Given that the aggressor needs to maintain a 1:2 bluff-to-value ratio, it means they can only bet 20 of these air combos as bluffs.

DID YOU KNOW?

The concept of *loss leaders* should not be confused with *range protection* which we will define later in this chapter. Often, GTO play requires that we include stronger hands in our checking ranges in order to prevent an opponent from generating exploits. However, the solver only does this if the EV of checking is *at least* as high as the EV of betting; it will never sacrifice EV in order to protect a range.

BOARD

HAND	STRATEGY	BET EV	CHECK EV
53o (bluff)	Bet: 44.4% Check: 55.6%	$0	$0
54o (bluff)	Bet: 44.4% Check: 55.6%	$0	$0

Since the aggressor's value hands can never lose, they would ideally just increase their river bet sizing. This would allow the aggressor to fire a larger portion of air hands as a bluff. We will assume, in this case, that the aggressor only has $100 left in their stack making this the maximum possible bet sizing.

If the aggressor can only fire 20 of their 45 air combos, this is the same as bluffing 20/45 or 44.4% of the time when holding a bluff. If we thought that the 44.4% mixing frequency in the above table initially looked random, we can now see that it has a very deliberate purpose: *making sure the bluff-to-value ratio of the bet remains balanced.*

Although the EV of betting and checking air hands is identical, employing mixed strategies is not optional in this case. The mixed strategies are *mandatory* in order to make sure the aggressor maintains the correct bluff-to-value ratio when betting the river.

LESSON 3: MIXED STRATEGIES = EQUIVALENT EV

Mixing is only an option when the EV of two or more lines is completely identical. If a solver is recommending a mixed strategy, it means the EV of the mixed lines must be identical. We therefore need to keep this in mind when analyzing solver output.

Players may sometimes assume that if a solver recommends a certain option at a higher frequency, then this option must be "better." In our example, the aggressor checks with air 56% of the time and bets with air 44% of the time. This does not mean that checking is a better option than betting: both actions are identical in terms of EV.

This rule holds true for even more extreme setups. Imagine a scenario where a hand is bet with a 95% frequency and only checked with a 5% frequency. Once again, this does not mean that betting is a better option than checking: both have the same expected value.

If one line legitimately did have a higher EV, the solver would always just take the higher EV option with a 100% frequency and there would be zero mixing in such a case.

SHOULD STRONG HANDS BE MIXED AS CHECKS?

Our *perfect polarization* solver model shows that the aggressor's value hands should always be bet and never checked. Does this mean that it is never correct for a strong hand to check the river in poker?

Let us first remember that our current model is incredibly simplified and does not represent all the nuances of a real river situation.

By making some tweaks to our solver model, it is possible to demonstrate that strong hands *should* be mixed into our checking ranges with some frequency depending on the scenario.

TWEAKING THE PERFECT POLARIZATION MODEL

Our new model will be identical to *Solver Model 1: Perfect Polarization* aside from one key difference: we will give the defender a number of busted draws alongside their pure bluff-catchers.

Assume that both players start out by playing the same way as in the previous model. Watching how the actions iterate can teach us lessons about how GTO strategies are formed.

Note that in this updated model, we will always refer to the out of position player as the *aggressor* and the in-position player as the *defender* (even though the defender could bet when checked to).

Step 1: The defender begins to realize that the aggressor is always folding after checking the river. The defender then exploits the aggressor by always bluffing the river with busted draws, and checking behind with their bluff-catchers.

Step 2: The aggressor begins to realize that the defender is bluffing a huge amount when checked to on the river. The aggressor calculates that they can now generate a higher expected value by checking value hands on the river and inducing a bluff.

Step 3: The defender suspects that the aggressor is simply not folding anymore after checking. So the defender starts reducing their bluffs.

Step 4: The aggressor realizes that the defender is not bluffing as often when checked to, and that checking value hands no longer maximizes EV. The aggressor shifts most value hands back into the betting range. However, since the defender has shown they are capable of exploiting an undefended checking range, the aggressor continues to check a percentage of value hands. It will no longer be +EV to try and push the exploit too far, since there will be a breaking point where the defender realizes they are being exploited and lowers the EV of the aggressor by countering.

Step 5: The defender does in fact realize that the aggressor is once again folding too much after checking (although not folding quite as often as before). The defender starts to bluff the river when checked (but not quite as aggressively as before). The defender knows that the aggressor is capable of countering if the bluff-to-value ratio gets too far out of line, so the defender does their best to subtly exploit the aggressor without making it too obvious.

Step 6: The aggressor is smart enough to notice that the defender is bluffing slightly more often than correct when checked to on the river. The aggressor then subtly shifts a few more value hands into their checking range. Perhaps the defender will not notice and will continue to over-bluff when checked to.

Step 7: The defender picks up on the fact that the aggressor is not folding quite often enough for bluffing to be profitable. The defender subtly starts bluffing less often than is correct, but does not push things as far as they did previously.

Step 8: The aggressor notices the small adjustment in the defender's bluff to value ratio and shifts a minuscule amount of value combos back to the betting range where their EV will be highest.

Step 9: The defender realizes that the aggressor is now over-folding the river by a minuscule amount after checking.

Notice how the two players iterate against each other, using smaller and smaller exploitative responses at each step. We might visualize this as displayed in the following diagram:

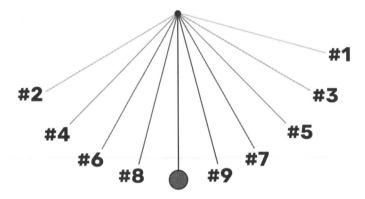

If the diagram represents smaller and smaller exploitative adjustments, what is represented by the red dot at the very center?

This is the point where there are no additional exploitative opportunities available for either player. Each player is completely balanced and cannot increase their win-rate by deviating from their current strategy.

In game theory lingo, this is referred to as a Nash Equilibrium.

NASH EQUILIBRIUM

This term describes the game state where no player can increase their win-rate by deviating. In poker terms, a Nash equilibrium is achieved when two players are playing perfect GTO poker against each other.

Note that the aggressor has no choice but to mix strong hands into their river checking range. If the aggressor fails to do so, the defender has an exploitative bluffing opportunity.

However, the aggressor cannot place *all* of their value hands into the checking range because:

- The aggressor will miss out on the additional EV that comes from value betting.

- The defender can stop bluffing as an exploit.

The only way to maximize the EV of every hand is for the aggressor to have a perfect mix of bets and checks with their strong holdings. Without this perfect mix, the defender can generate an exploitative counter-strategy, which in turn lowers the EV of the aggressor's hands.

Thus, we see that mixing is a crucial part of maximizing EV.

AGAINST NON-ADJUSTING PLAYERS

If our opponent is not capable of finding exploitative counter-strategies, mixed strategies lose much of their value. If the EV of betting and checking is the same, betting and checking in any proportion will result in the exact same win-rate against a non-adjusting opponent.

However, we often find the EV of various actions is less likely to be the same against opponents who fail to adjust. Exploitative poker often makes heavy use of pure strategies as a result and does not make use of mixed strategies as often as a GTO approach.

Against very good players, we might not be able to get away with overly-obvious pure strategy exploits. The two players in our above model tried to exploit as hard as possible while still flying below their opponent's radar.

Trying to exploit our opponent *too hard* will actually lower our EV if they are capable of quickly deploying the relevant counter-strategy.

CONFIRMING WITH THE SOLVER

So far we have had the audacity to make a lot of claims about a solver model that we have yet to run. Let us see if we can confirm our assumptions by making use of *Solver Model 2 - Imperfect Polarization - Air Heavy Defender*.

BOARD

AGGRESSOR (OOP)	DEFENDER (IP)
(13x13 range grid)	(13x13 range grid)
KQs-KJs,63s-62s,54s-52s, KQo-KJo,63o-62o,54o-52o	T9s-T7s,T9o-T7o, 98o-97o,87o

Note that the defender now has a number of busted gutshots alongside their Tx bluff-catchers. The busted gutshots will currently chop at showdown against the air hands in the aggressor's range and may benefit from trying to fold the aggressor off a chop when checked to.

Here is the result of the aggressor's new river strategy:

HAND TYPE	COMBOS	BET %	CHECK %
Value Hands	40	75%	25%
Air	45	33.3%	66.7%
All Hands	85	52.9%	47.1%

We can confirm that the aggressor is now required to protect their checking range with some strong holdings. This is a concept we will refer to as *range protection*.

RANGE PROTECTION

The term range protection refers to the inclusion of some stronger holdings in checking and small bet-sizing ranges, so that those ranges can defend themselves. However, it is never correct to sacrifice EV in order to protect a range. The EV of checking (or betting small) must be *at least* as high as the other available options.

The aggressor still maintains a perfect 1:2 bluff-to-value ratio when betting. The aggressor also defends exactly half of the time after checking the river (and facing a pot-sized bet), preventing the defender from being able to make auto-profitable bluffs.

Especially observant students might notice that the aggressor checks the river with a range of 10 value combos and 30 air combos. You might then wonder why the aggressor is not folding 75% of the time to a river bet. This is because the solver model has the aggressor check/calling with 10 air combos for the chop, creating the perfect folding frequency of exactly 50%.

DID YOU KNOW?

It might seem like some hugely weird coincidence that the EV of checking a certain hand ends up being precisely the same as the EV of betting. *What are the chances, right?* And yet we see this type of thing everywhere in GTO play.

Of course, it is not a coincidence. Our GTO opponent is deliberately making us indifferent between our available options in the proposed model.

THE GEMS

- We should always play every hand in our range at its maximum EV.

- Mixed strategies are a requirement for GTO play.

- Mixed strategies are only used when the EV of two (or more) lines is the same.

- We often need to protect weak ranges with some stronger holdings (a concept known as *range protection*).

- Mixed strategies are not that important against weak opponents.

- There may be a limit to how far we can push exploits against advanced opposition.

FINAL ADVICE

Avoid getting overwhelmed with complex mixed frequencies. Occasionally mixing up the way you play hands can make you much tougher to play against.

MULTIPLE BET SIZES ARE MANDATORY

Good poker players have long attempted (and sometimes succeeded) in harnessing the power of bet-sizing tells. The idea is that the bet sizes our opponents choose may give away important information about the types of hands they are holding.

As a simple example, imagine an opponent who always bets full-pot when strong, but half-pot with weak hands and bluffs. Generating a winning strategy would be quite simple here. We would simply fold our bluff-catchers when facing large bets, and defend actively against the smaller bet size.

If you are thinking that telegraphing clear information about our hand through bet sizing does not sound very 'GTO', you would be 100% correct! It is about as GTO as eating an Oreo every time we make the nuts.

So how exactly are we supposed to avoid giving away information through our bet sizings?

A SINGLE-SIZE SOLUTION?

The logical first question that many poker players ask is: *What happens if we simply bet every single hand with the same bet sizing?*

At first glance, it might seem that the problem is solved. After all, our opponent is going to have absolutely no idea what type of hand we hold if we always pick the same sizing.

Historically, many players believed that this was the definition of *balance* in poker.

Unfortunately, this is not a good definition of balance, since we can prove quite easily that a single-sizing strategy can be exploited.

Let us look at an example:

Example: The aggressor always bets $50 into a $100 pot on the river with a perfectly polarized range. They bluff 50% of the time and value bet 50% of the time.

Take a moment to try and answer these three questions.

- Is the aggressor balanced here?

- Can we exploit the aggressor here?

- If yes, *how* can we exploit the aggressor here?

It is certainly true that the defender has no clue what the aggressor has at any given moment. It is a 50/50 coin flip whether the aggressor has a bluff or a value hand. However, this does not mean that the aggressor is balanced.

With a half-pot bet size, the aggressor should be employing a 1:3 bluff-to-value ratio. The aggressor should be bluffing 25% of the time and value betting the other 75% of the time. This is because the defender is being offered 3:1 pot odds.

As it stands, the defender can exploit the aggressor by calling with all bluff-catchers, because the aggressor is bluffing too frequently from a GTO standpoint.

We clearly need a new definition of balance, because always using the same bet sizing is not quite ticking the boxes.

A DEFINITION OF BALANCE

Let us look at a more accurate definition of balance in poker:

DID YOU KNOW?

The term *"balanced"* is often used interchangeably with *"unexploitable"* when discussing poker in a GTO context. Similarly, an *"unbalanced"* strategy typically refers to a non-GTO strategy that is exploitable.

BALANCE

A byproduct of playing every hand in our range at maximum EV against a perfect GTO opponent.

Do not worry too much if this definition does not immediately resonate. Expect a 3 AM *"aha moment"* an unspecified number of days from now.

In the meantime, there are a couple of key lessons that we can extract from this definition.

GTO PLAY IS THE BEST EXPLOITATIVE STRATEGY AGAINST A PERFECT GTO OPPONENT

Some sources appear to imply that exploitative and GTO poker are opposite ends of the spectrum, and that each represents a completely different approach to the game of poker. It is not uncommon for debates to break out online regarding whether the best poker players should use GTO or exploitative strategies.

But what *is* exploitative poker? It is a strategy that always seeks to maximize our EV through exploitation, regardless of whether it makes us *unbalanced* in the process. What happens if we try to maximize our EV against a perfect GTO opponent? We end up playing perfect GTO poker ourselves.

In other words, GTO poker is a type of exploitative poker.

This frees us enough to understand that the sole objective of any poker player should be to exploit their opponent as hard as possible. GTO poker is simply just one manifestation of exploitative poker. It is the scenario in which both players are so good at exploitation that neither has any incentive to deviate from their current strategy.

BALANCED PLAY IS A BYPRODUCT, NOT OUR MAIN AREA OF FOCUS

When we exploit weak opposition, the end result is that we end up playing an unbalanced game (albeit for a good reason). When we exploit a perfect GTO opponent, the end result is that we automatically play a perfectly balanced game.

In other words, balance is a *byproduct* of playing exploitative poker well. Attempting to make balance our main area of focus is actually approaching the problem backward. We are not trying to be balanced purely for the sake of being balanced.

If we instead focus on developing strategies that maximize our EV, the degree of balance in our strategy will simply be a response to how skilled our opponent is. Generally speaking, the more skilled our opponent is, the more balanced our own game will become when playing the highest-EV counter-strategy.

If we push exploits too far against good opposition, we run the risk of them being able to efficiently counter and significantly reduce the EV of our overall gameplan. We gave an example of this in the previous chapter, in which each player adjusted their strategy to exploit the other. In that example, neither player was *trying* to be balanced. However, their game plans automatically and progressively became more balanced as they competed.

BALANCED PLAY MEANS MULTIPLE BET SIZINGS

While the idea of only using a single bet size may have initially appeared logical, balanced play actually requires the use of multiple bet sizes in order to maximize EV. We can illustrate this with a simple thought experiment.

Imagine a simple river situation where we are the aggressor with two different types of value hands in our range:

Nuts: This is the stone-cold nuts and the defender can never win when they call.

Thin Value: This is a reasonably strong value hand, but not invincible. Although the defender can call with second-best holdings, they will also have some stronger hands in their defense range.

What does your intuition tell you about our bet-sizing plan here?

A logical answer would be:

- Our nutted holdings maximize their EV by betting large.

- Our thin value holdings maximize their EV by betting small.

- Bonus points if you mentioned that the smaller sizing might need some range protection.

Now imagine we try to force all of these holdings into a single bet size. We run into one of the following two problems:

If we always use the small sizing, our thin value hands would do well, but our nutted holdings would be missing out on extracting additional EV with a larger bet size.

If we always use the large sizing, our nutted hands would do well, but our thin-value hands would lose too many chips in situations when they are behind, lowering their overall EV as bets.

It is actually *impossible* for us to maximize our EV by only using just one bet size here.

The major takeaway is that, not only does using multiple sizings not make us unbalanced, using multiple sizings is *mandatory* if we want a balanced strategy.

A SIMPLE MULTIPLE-SIZINGS SOLVER MODEL

Let us set up a very simple solver model based on the above premise.

It is a river model with the following features:

- The aggressor has some strong value hands, some thin value hands, and some bluffs.

- The defender has a selection of bluff-catchers along with some slightly stronger hands.

- The defender's bluff-catchers only beat the aggressor's bluffs.

- The defender's stronger holdings generally beat the aggressor's thin value hands but lose to his strong value hands.

- The solver has the ability to bet either $50 or $150 into a $100 pot (i.e., a smaller bet sizing and a larger bet sizing).

If you want to follow along with the GTO+ solve, load the *Solver Model 3: Multiple Sizings Demo*.

BOARD

AGGRESSOR (OOP)	DEFENDER (IP)

AA,77,33-22,AKs,A9s-A8s,A6s,A2s,98s, 86s-85s,65s,AKo,A9o,A2o,98o,96o,86o-85o,65o

AQs-AJs,A7s,J7s,T7s,97s,87s, AQo-AJo,A7o,J7o,T7o,97o,87o

Full House+	16 combos	Top Pair+	33 combos
Nuts		Stronger Hands	
Top Pair	30 combos	Middle Pair	48 combos
Thin Value		Bluffcatchers	
Air	76 combos		

After running the solve, we get the heat map below which shows the distribution of the different actions the solver takes. This type of output is commonly used by solvers to quickly display all strategic options at a glance.

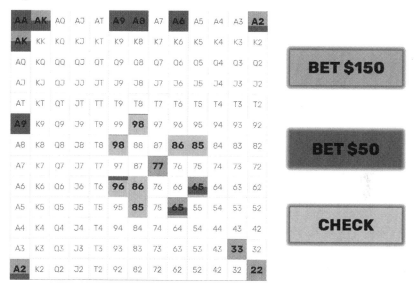

We can see that the solver does make use of both different bet sizings, as predicted. The half-pot sizing is used 30.7% of the time while the overbet sizing is used 21.7% of the time.

Keep in mind that the solver will only use a certain bet sizing if it is possible to maximize the EV of that player's strategy by doing so. If this is not the case, the solver simply will not use that bet size.

ANALYSIS OF CHOSEN SIZINGS

Let us see if we can get a better understanding of which sizes are being chosen by the solver and why. We can break the hands down into two categories, those that use *pure strategies* and those that use *mixed strategies*.

CATEGORY 1: PURE STRATEGIES

77, 33, 22 (full houses and quads). These all use a pure overbet strategy. This makes sense since these hands can never be beaten.

Weak Ax (one pair). These hands all use a pure strategy with the small sizing. This also makes sense, because these hands do not want to lose too much if they run into the stronger holdings in the defender's range.

AA (full house). Perhaps the most interesting pure strategy result here is for pocket Aces. This hand uses the small bet sizing with a 100% frequency despite never losing to any of the hands in the defender's range. The reasons for this will be discussed in Chapter 11.

It is true that smaller bet sizings (and checks) potentially need some stronger hands in them for range protection. However, this is likely *not* the main reason why AA is a pure small bet within our current model.

CATEGORY 2: MIXED STRATEGIES

AKo & AKs (strong top pairs). These are mixed across both of the small bet and overbet lines. This means the EV of both lines must be the same.

Take a moment and try to answer the question:

Why is the solver seemingly indifferent here?

Looking closely at the model, we see that AK occupies a unique location in terms of how the ranges of both players interact. Unlike the other hands in the aggressor's thin value category, AKo beats some of the defender's stronger hands (AJ and AQ). However, unlike the aggressor's strongest holdings, AK loses to the defender's A7 (two pair).

AK is therefore solidly in the middle ground. It is not an obvious small bet like weak Ax hands, but it is clearly not an obvious overbet candidate since it loses to some of the hands in the defender's range (i.e. A7). Consequently, it makes sense that this is a hand the solver would choose to mix.

However, this does not explain why A2s and A2o are also mixed into the small bet-sizing range. These seem like obvious candidates for overbets since they can never lose to any of the defender's range. They must share some similarities with pocket Aces, which again we will explore in Chapter 11.

The air hands are also mixed strategies, for reasons that should now be familiar. The solver mixes the air hands in order to maintain a balanced bluff-to-value ratio across both the small sizing and overbet sizing.

The solver does not select the air hands at random as in earlier models, but favors certain bluff combos such as 65.

THE GEMS

- It is impossible to play GTO poker without the use of multiple bet sizes.

- The sole objective of any poker player should be to exploit their opponent as hard as possible.

- Without multiple sizings, some of our hands will not be able to maximize their EV by playing at their preferred sizing.

- Strong holdings often bet large, but they also need to be used in smaller bet sizing ranges for range protection.

- Bluffs should appear in all bet-sizing ranges using the appropriate bluff-to-value ratio.

FINAL ADVICE

Do not be afraid to vary your bet sizings if there is a good reason for it. Remember that using multiple sizings does not necessarily mean that your opponents will be able to exploit you.

GEM #6

EQUITY DISTRIBUTIONS

In the early days of players attempting to use GTO strategies, virtually every decision was driven by the pot equity that one range had against another range.

> ## EQUITY
>
> Equity, or *pot equity*, refers to how often a hand or range can expect to win at showdown if there is no further betting action. It is often thought of as a player's rightful share of the current pot, based on the strength of their hand or range.

Even today, it is common to hear comments such as:

- *"Our range has more equity, so we should bet at a high frequency here."*

- *"Villain's range has more equity, so we should be checking a lot here."*

These statements sound logical, and some of the time they might even be true.

However, it is fairly trivial to demonstrate with a GTO solver that these statements are also downright incorrect in a large number of scenarios. It is simple to construct a solver model where a range with more equity is supposed to check and a range with less equity is supposed to bet.

Things become even more problematic when players try to determine the optimal bet size they should be using based on the overall pot equity of their range.

For example, which of these statements is true?

- *"Our range has the most equity, so we should bet large."*

- *"Our range has the most equity, so we should bet small."*

Both are statements commonly made by serious poker players, but surely they cannot *both* be true. So which is correct?

As it turns out, none of the previous four statements are technically correct. *Why not?*

WHY EQUITY IS NOT THE FULL STORY

The reason why the previous statements are incorrect is that it is impossible to determine a GTO strategy if we only know our pot equity.

For example, imagine a situation where our range has roughly 50% pot equity against our opponent's range. It might seem like this gives us a lot of information about how the ranges stack up, but in truth, it tells us virtually nothing.

The following table lists three possible configurations where both ranges have *exactly* 50% pot equity.

SCENARIO	PLAYER 1 (50% EQUITY)	PLAYER 2 (50% EQUITY)
1	Same range as Player 2.	Same range as Player 1.
2	The top 50% of hands have 100% equity while the bottom 50% of hands have 0% equity against Player 2.	Every hand has exactly 50% equity against Player 1's range.
3	A random selection of hands that just-so-happen to have exactly 50% equity against Player 2's range.	A random selection of hands that just-so-happen to have exactly 50% equity against Player 1's range.

On reflection, there are a huge number of possible situations where each player's range can have roughly 50% pot equity.

If pot equity actually mattered in determining our betting strategy, we would expect to see similar overall strategies being employed across the three different scenarios in our table. What we *actually* see is the solver employing very different strategies depending on the exact details of each scenario.

This is because a GTO strategy is not so much based on how much equity a range has, but rather on *how the equity is distributed*.

EQUITY DISTRIBUTION

The term *equity distribution* refers to how equity is distributed across a range in comparison to another range.

EQUITY DISTRIBUTION

This can be visualized in what is known as an equity distribution graph.

An equity distribution graph is a visual representation of the equities of hands in two competing ranges. It does so by measuring the equity of every single hand in range 1 versus the entirety of range 2, and vice versa.

Equity is displayed vertically on the left-hand side (y-axis) while the hand location in the overall range is displayed horizontally along the bottom (x-axis).

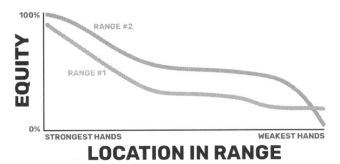

Equity distribution graphs may sound complex, but they are fairly straightforward once one understands how they work.

Bear in mind that not all GTO solvers will provide the ability to see an equity distribution graph. We might instead need to make use of an equity calculator.

The GTO+ solver can automatically export hands to the Flopzilla Pro equity calculator, allowing us to instantly see the equity distribution for every situation in the solves that we run.

As an example, let us take a look at the equity distribution of the earlier perfect polarization model.

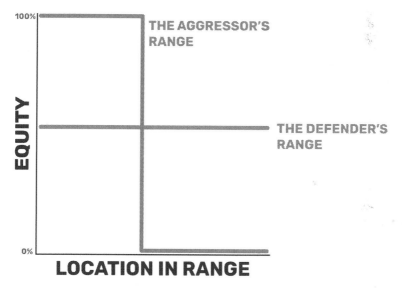

The polarized range starts at the top left of the equity distribution graph. These are the aggressor's value hands which individually each have 100% pot equity against the defender's entire range.

At about the halfway point the aggressor's line falls sharply and intersects the defender's horizontal line. At the bottom right of the equity distribution graph we see the aggressor's bluffs, which individually each have 0% pot equity against the defender's entire range of pure bluff-catchers.

The defender's equity line is completely horizontal and appears at around half of the height of the overall equity distribution graph. This is because every single hand in the defender's range has roughly 50% equity against the aggressor's entire range (52.941% equity to be exact).

The defender's range can be referred to as a *condensed range*.

> ## CONDENSED RANGE
>
> A range that contains primarily middling hands that lose to the value hands against a polarized range, but beats the bluffs. Technically, *polarized* and *condensed* ranges should always appear in pairs, as it is impossible to have one without the other.

A MORE REALISTIC DISTRIBUTION

The previous graph is based on the model of perfect polarization which is an overly-simplified version of how poker actually works.

Instead, it is more common to see ranges that have strong elements of polarization but are not *perfectly* polarized.

The following equity distribution graph is taken from a more advanced model (*Solver Model 4: A More Realistic Multi-Street Solve*) which we will discuss a little later in this book.

Without knowing the precise situation, can we conclude anything by looking at this equity distribution graph?

We once again see the pattern where an equity line starts higher up on the left-hand side of the graph, but then vertically intersects the second line, and finally finishes up in the lower-right corner. This is another example of a conjugate pair of polarized and condensed ranges..

Since this is taken from a river situation, the polarized range will typically be played by the aggressor, while the condensed range will be played by the defender.

In this more realistic depiction of a polarized range, many of the value hands have less than 100% equity against the condensed range. Put another way, some of the value hands in the aggressor's range may occasionally lose to even stronger holdings in the defender's range.

We also notice that, since the aggressor's equity line starts slightly higher up on the left of the equity graph, their range contains hands that the defender cannot currently beat (and will never be able to beat since this is a river situation). This is an important principle in GTO poker, and is referred to as having the *nutted equity distribution*.

NUTTED EQUITY DISTRIBUTION

A range is said to have the nutted equity distribution when it contains hands that are so strong that the other range can never beat them (at least not without additional cards being dealt). E.g., if Player 1 has KK and QQ in their range on a KQ5 flop, but Player 2 does not, then we can say that Player 1 has the nutted equity distribution.

UNDERSTANDING RANGE ADVANTAGE

The term *range advantage* simply means that one range is more desirable or more profitable than another. Historically, however, range advantage has been used almost exclusively to indicate that one range has more pot equity than another.

RANGE ADVANTAGE

This term should *ideally* mean that one range is more favorable or more profitable than another, regardless of the ranges' overall pot equity. However, perhaps misleadingly, the term is often used to indicate that one range simply has more pot equity than another range. This is despite pot equity often not being the most important aspect in determining whether one range is more profitable than another.

Solver analysis teaches us that it is possible for one range to be better even if it has less pot equity. As a simple example of this, polarized ranges are more profitable than condensed ranges as a general rule.

In *Solver Model 1: Perfect Polarization*, the polarized aggressor's range has 47% pot equity while the defender's range has 53%. It might be tempting to say that the defender has a range advantage simply because their equity is higher.

If we look at the expected value of each player, however, we can see that this would be a misleading use of terminology. Out of the $100 in the pot, the polarized aggressor walks away with $70.59 on average while the defender walks away with the remaining $29.41.

It is arguably more accurate to say that the aggressor has the range advantage here, since their equity is distributed more favorably (i.e., it is a polarized distribution which translates into higher earnings).

Holding the nutted equity distribution also confers a big advantage to a range. This is because having the nutted equity distribution allows us to construct polarized ranges more cleanly.

Although the stronger holdings often get the most focus, it is possible for range advantages to also occur towards the middle (or even bottom) of an equity distribution.

For example, let us break down the equity distribution for *Solver Model 4: A More Realistic Multi-Street Solve*. We will split it loosely into three categories: top, middle, and bottom. We will also continue to identify the polarized range with the aggressor and the condensed range with the defender.

SECTION OF RANGE	ADVANTAGE
Top	The stronger holdings run close in equity, although the aggressor has the nutted equity advantage.
Middle	The aggressor has a significant advantage in the middle of the ranges.
Bottom	The defender has an advantage lower down in the ranges because their worst holdings are much better than the aggressor's.

Conceivably, it is possible for one range to have the nutted equity distribution, but the second range to end up being better because it is significantly stronger in the deeper parts of the range.

Understanding exactly how two ranges stack up like this gives us a much more reliable way of predicting what a GTO strategy looks like, along with its associated frequencies and bet sizings.

THE GEMS

- It is impossible to know the correct GTO strategy by only considering the raw pot equity of our range.

- The range that has the most pot equity is not necessarily the most profitable to play.

- We need to consider the *equity distribution* of both players' ranges.

- Some aspects of a range are more valuable than raw equity, such as having the polarized range and/or having the nutted equity distribution.

FINAL ADVICE

Avoid getting bogged down with trying to consider equity distributions in too much detail while actually playing. If you can simply recognize when a polarized and condensed range pair is being formed, this will go a long way in helping you to figure out the best strategy.

ATTACKING WITH POLARIZED RANGES

In the game of chess, expert players spend a considerable amount of time studying the final stages of the game, known as the endgame.

By understanding which endgame board positions are favorable, they can make decisions in the earlier stages of the game that slowly lead them towards a winning endgame position.

In poker, our endgame is the river. Our end goal, where possible, is to reach the river with a well-constructed polarized range since we know these are more profitable on average than condensed ranges. Of course, it is not entirely our decision since it will depend on the community cards. Sometimes we will have no choice but to play a condensed range.

By making careful decisions about our range on the earlier streets, however, we can funnel ourselves towards river situations where we have a well-constructed polarized range as frequently as possible.

EARLIER STREET PLAY

Clear pairs of polarized and condensed ranges only really exist on the river (and occasionally on very dry turns).

It is still common to use terms such as "polarized" and "condensed" to describe earlier street situations, and we will do that in this book. What we are really seeing on flops and turns, though, is an early version of those specific equity distributions as they begin to form. We do not see them in their purest manifestations until the river.

Discussing a polarized range on the flop is like looking at the range through a distorted lens. We see *some* of the basic characteristics of a polarized range beginning to form, but the outline of the range still lacks definition. There could still be a number of mid-strength hands within this polarized range for example. We will expand on *how* these ranges form in the next chapter.

These characteristics of the newly-formed ranges are still often enough for us to be able to make solid predictions regarding what a solver strategy would look like, and whether we should start working towards a condensed or polarized river range with the various hands that we hold.

PREDICTING BET SIZING

In the previous chapter, our analysis of river situations demonstrated that it is impossible to predict bet sizings by looking purely at range-versus-range pot equity. It is the equity distribution that gives us clues regarding which bet sizings will be incentivized. We will use similar logic for flop and turn decisions.

As a general guide, a range that has the *nutted equity distribution* will often take on the role of aggressor, and will make use of large bet sizes while working towards a polarized river range.

Simply put, if a range has lots of nutted equity holdings, a large bet sizing is used more frequently.

Unlike a *perfectly* polarized range, the aggressor will hold a selection of fairly strong hands that can extract value, but will still lose to a number of hands in the defender's range. These are candidates for using smaller bet sizes.

Since the defender might be able to exploit betting ranges that do not contain any nutted hands, the aggressor is required to mix some nutted combos into the smaller bet-sizing ranges for range protection.

If a range has a large density of thinner value hands that prefer small bet sizings, a larger number of the stronger hands are required for range protection. A range that is more polarized, and contains fewer mid-strength hands, can thus use the larger bet sizes at a higher frequency, given that fewer of the strong holdings are required as smaller bet sizes for range protection.

BETTING FREQUENCY

Our analysis of river situations in the previous chapter also revealed that it is impossible to accurately predict the correct betting frequency purely from range-versus-range equity. This rule also holds true for flop and turn scenarios.

This is not to say that there will be *zero* correlation. Looking at the big picture, ranges with more pot equity *do* bet more frequently on average. Being aware of our pot equity can still be worthwhile. But it is definitely not a given that a range is bet more frequently (or even at all) just because it is a favorite in terms of pot equity.

It is probably more accurate to say that a range is bet at a high frequency simply if it contains many hands that have the right characteristics for betting.

Taking a simplified approach, there are two main reasons why we bet individual hands:

- Building the pot in case we win (value hands and semi-bluffs)

- Folding villain off of their share of pot equity (bluffs and mid-strength hands).

Ranges aside; any time we are betting or raising with an individual hand, it is worth considering which of these two categories our hand fits into.

Regarding the second point, even top pair hands that are strong enough to extract thin value on the flop and turn may generate a higher EV when our opponent folds their equity share rather than makes the

DID YOU KNOW?

Players used to believe that the two reasons for betting were a.) extracting value (which means we must have over 50% pot equity if our opponent calls) and b.) bluffing; that is, trying to get our opponent to fold better hands.

Mid-strength hands should nearly always check according to this model, since they are not strong enough to value bet but are too strong to bluff. Solver work has demonstrated that this model is inaccurate. Mid-strength hands should actually still bet in certain circumstances.

call. It simply depends on *how much pot equity* is being folded. It is the difference between splitting the pot up almost evenly when our opponent calls, or taking down the entire pot when they fold.

The larger the amount of equity we can fold out, the more likely it is we prefer a fold than a call. Betting for the sole purpose of folding our opponent off their share of the pot is a concept usually referred to as *equity denial*.

EQUITY DENIAL

Betting to capitalize on the fact that our opponent will fold out their equity share. This is typically done with weak and mid-strength hands, despite the fact that these combos may already be the best hand with some frequency.

SIMPLE SOLVER MODELS

Let us put what we have learned thus far into practice and predict how frequently certain models will bet on the flop, and which bet sizes they will typically prefer.

In the following flop situations, we are out of position, and the analysis is based upon a simple solver model that makes use of a small and large bet size.

A loose description of the equity distribution is usually enough to begin making solid predictions regarding GTO strategy. However, as an extra option, it is possible to see the precise ranges by downloading the available GTO+ solver models.

SCENARIO: NUTTED EQUITY DISTRIBUTION
AND SOME AIR, NOTHING IN THE MIDDLE

Solver Model 5 - Nutted Equity Distribution & Not Too Much Trash

This is the perfect example of a range that likes to bet, since we can formulate a polarized range by the river very easily. Flop ranges are not usually this polarized so soon, but we have kept the models extremely simple for clarity.

Because our range does not contain too much trash, we can bet most of it without becoming too bluff-heavy on the later streets.

The solver uses the large bet sizing with a 95% frequency and never uses the small sizing. The high betting frequency might seem surprising when we consider that the overall range only has 36% pot equity, but this is the power of a polarized range!

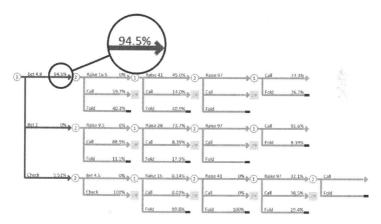

The 5% checking range is pure air with zero strong hands for protection. Range protection is not required in this case because our opponent never bets when checked to.

If we tweak the model by adding some trash hands into our opponent's range, the solver then protects the flop checking range with some strong hands. The solver still bets very frequently overall, but not quite as often since some of the value hands get checked.

SCENARIO: NUTTED EQUITY DISTRIBUTION
WITH A LARGE AMOUNT OF AIR

Solver Model 6 - Nutted Equity Distribution With Too Much Trash

The solver's betting frequency now drops dramatically to around 17%. It is simply impossible for the solver to bet all of the trash hands without becoming overly air-heavy by the turn and river.

Remember, our goal is to set up a well-balanced polarized range by the river. It is better to ditch most of those very trashy hands sooner rather than later. Thus, the solver has no choice but to check trash hands with a very high frequency.

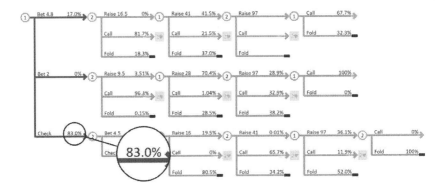

Since the value hands are nutted, the solver always picks the larger bet sizing when betting.

Assuming we check the river, the solver advises our opponent to bet in position despite having a condensed range. It seems condensed ranges do not always play purely for defense. More on this in the next chapter.

SCENARIO: NO NUTTED EQUITY DISTRIBUTION, BUT BIG RANGE ADVANTAGE DEEPER IN THE RANGE WITH SOME AIR

Solver Model 7 - Deep Range Advantage Without Nutted Equity

It is a little harder to start forming a clean polarized range here, since we do not have the nutted equity distribution. If we bet too large, we run the risk of losing too many chips against the stronger hands in our opponent's range.

That said, there are still plenty of second-best hands with which our opponent can call if we size our bets carefully.

Betting value hands also allows us to fire some of our air hands on the flop. Remember that GTO play wants us to continue as frequently as is mathematically possible.

As anticipated, the solver only makes use of the smaller bet sizing and fires around 24% of the time.

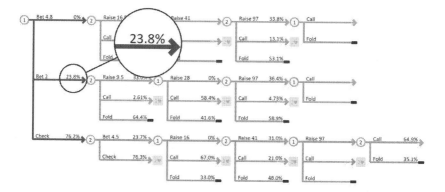

If we increase the number of weaker hands in villain's range (decreasing the defender's overall equity), the solver will advise that we use a higher betting frequency (while continuing to use the smaller bet sizing). Conversely, if we decrease the number of villain's weaker hands, the solver will start to recommend that we check the flop with a 100% frequency.

We can see that with this specific model, there is a correlation between pot equity and betting frequency. We are more likely to see this type of correlation when dealing with a deeper range advantage as opposed to a nutted range advantage.

SCENARIO: RANGE WITH THE NUTTED EQUITY DISTRIBUTION, BUT SIGNIFICANT RANGE DISADVANTAGE DEEPER IN THE RANGE

Solver Model 8 - Nutted Equity With Deep Range Disadvantage

The equity of our range is now only around 35% due to the deep range disadvantage. The lack of pot equity, caused by this weakness in the deeper part of our range, explains why the solver bets with a very low frequency here.

Despite this, we have some hands in our range that have the correct characteristics for betting, even though our range's overall pot equity is low.

First, we have the nutted equity distribution which allows the solver to make use of the larger bet sizing with some frequency (4%).

Second, some of our non-nut holdings are still strong enough to dominate the weaker holdings in villain's range. For this reason, the solver also makes use of the small bet-sizing range 8% of the time.

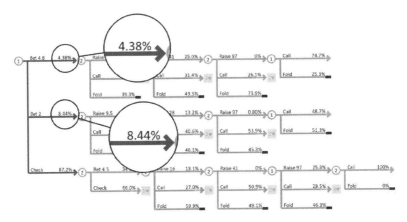

Although our strongest holdings appear mostly in the large bet-sizing range, the solver mixes them into the smaller sizing for range protection. Our weaker middling hands are 100% pure checks however since they do not function well as part of the larger bet-sizing range.

THE GEMS

- A nutted equity distribution usually means large bet sizes.

- An advantage deeper in the range usually means smaller bet sizes.

- We bet at a higher frequency if our range contains many hands that have the correct characteristics for betting.

- Hands bet either to build a pot or for equity denial.

- Pot equity is more likely to be correlated with betting frequency for deeper range advantages.

FINAL ADVICE

Why not consider getting your hands dirty and digging into some solver models if you have not done so already? A great start is to load up the existing GTO+ models and see what happens to the results if you tweak some of the parameters. Download all of the GTO+ models mentioned in this book by going to www.gtogems.com/solverfiles.

If you do not already own GTO+, you can purchase a copy by going to www.gtogems.com/solver.

GEM #8

DEFENDING WITH CONDENSED RANGES

Sometimes we have no choice but to work towards a condensed range by the river. Our opponent may be playing aggressively and we have mostly mid-strength hands in our range. There is nothing inherently wrong with this; sometimes it is simply correct from a GTO standpoint to play as the defender.

If we have the nutted equity distribution, we raise our strongest holdings when facing bets and adopt the role of polarized aggressor. In contrast, condensed ranges are forced to play quite passively, either calling or folding.

With a perfect polarization model, a condensed range should never bet into a polarized range at all. This is because the polarized range would only ever call with hands that beat the condensed range.

However, things are not so straightforward on earlier streets, especially the flop. It can be difficult to easily identify polarized/condensed range pairs when both ranges appear to have a little bit of everything.

EARLIER STREET PLAY

On the flop, it can be difficult initially to detect if a polarized and condensed range pair has begun to form. Even if we see the first outline of a condensed range taking shape, there will be a large number of imperfections relative to a true condensed range.

A true condensed range is supposed to contain purely middling hand strengths. But especially on the flop, there will be a number of much stronger and weaker hands in the range.

This means that the condensed range will still contain some holdings that want to bet. The air hands might ideally like to bet/raise as a bluff/ semi-bluff. Meanwhile, the stronger holdings may be good enough that they are incentivized to try and extract value, or bet for equity denial.

As the hand progresses, the condensed range will become more clearly defined and contain a larger proportion of mid-strength hands. The stronger and weaker hands "leave" the range by betting or raising, and attempting to form their own polarized range by the river. The remaining range, which plays passively by checking and calling, ends up containing an increasing proportion of mid-strength hands as we approach the river.

However, even if a condensed range has formed sufficiently to contain mostly mid-strength hands by the turn, perfect polarization does not really exist (apart from some extremely contrived models we might create).

This is because the river card still has the potential to change which range has the nutted equity distribution or the most pot equity. Sometimes a player who is initially heading towards a condensed river range as the defender may be required to take over the role of aggressor, by catching a turn or river card which connects very well with their range.

If the formation of polarized and condensed ranges over the course of hand seems abstract at this stage, do not worry too much. An example hand might help to see how the formation of these ranges takes place in practice.

IDENTIFYING CONDENSED RANGES

Take a hand example with 100bb effective stacks where the SB steals for 3bb, the BB 3-bets to 10bb, and the SB calls. The SB check/calls a 3/4-pot c-bet on AK5r. The SB check/calls a half-pot bet on the turn.

And the SB check/calls a half-pot all-in on the river.

PREFLOP/FLOP

Even after calling the BB's 3-bet and seeing the AK5 flop, the SB's range starts to display elements of being condensed, mostly because it lacks the nutted equity distribution.

The BB has hands like AA, KK, AK while the SB does not usually have these hands, since they would have 4-bet preflop. SB has more middling holdings such as A2-AJs, middling pocket pairs, and Kxs.

Even so, it would not be true to say that SB's range *only* contains middling hands. Holdings like 55 and A5s may have called preflop and are stronger than some of the BB's value hands. The SB also has some air, such as mid-suited connectors/gappers, that have completely missed the flop.

It would be a stretch to describe the BB's range as polarized at this stage, since the BB holds so many mid-strength hands like Kx, 5x, and pocket pairs below a King.

FLOP

The picture of both ranges becomes even clearer when BB fires a continuation bet (c-bet) on the flop.

Although mid-strength holdings may *occasionally* fire a continuation bet on the flop for equity denial reasons (e.g., 5x type holdings), most of them would check behind rather than c-bet.

Think about hands such as Kx and pocket pairs below a Queen. Although the solver occasionally mixes these hands, they mostly get checked behind.

Strong value hands like AK are mostly c-bet, with the exception that some value hands are checked for range protection purposes. The BB will also fire a selection of semi-bluffs, such as QJ, QT, JT gutshots, and backdoor-equity holdings like 9♠8♠.

When the SB *just calls* against the continuation bet, this has a further condensing effect on their range. First, the SB is required to fold their complete air along with pairs weaker than a King. The SB's calling range will thus contain a large number of mid-strength hands like Ax and Kx (although they are also still required to defend a chunk of gutshots).

A human SB player may also elect to check/raise holdings like 55 and A5s for value, although it is worth noting that many solvers do not advise the SB check-raise at all in this spot.

Going to the turn, we are starting to see the polarized and condensed ranges forming.

TURN

By the time the BB bets the turn, their range really begins to look polarized. The BB mostly has either a good Ax-type hand, or some type of bluff/semi-bluff. That said, there are still some middling hands that might fire a second barrel for protection. A holding like 54s, 76s or 87s may conceivably 3-bet preflop and fire both the flop and turn for equity denial benefits.

As for the SB, a number of the draws will now be forced to fold when facing the turn barrel. In fact, it is mostly just the combo draws like Q♦J♦ that continue at this stage. The rest of the calling range will be almost exclusively Ax or Kx hands. Any slightly stronger hands remaining within the range (e.g., 55 or AQo) may elect to raise at this stage, further condensing the SB's check/calling range.

RIVER

By the time the BB bets the river in this scenario, we usually have fairly neat polarization occurring. BB's value betting range will include holdings like AQ and stronger (occasionally AJ). It will also bet anything that completely bricks, along with some low pairs that are turned into bluffs.

The SB's calling range will be mostly Ax hands, although the SB occasionally has combos that beat some of the BBs river value bets such as K8s and A2s (which will also call). Thus we see that even when fairly neat polarization occurs, it is rarely perfect. The value hands in a polarized river betting range can still potentially lose some of the time.

SIMPLE SOLVER MODELS ON THE FLOP

Let us spend a few moments analyzing some flop-specific models with condensed ranges using both small and large sizes. Our goal is to see how equity, vulnerability, and betting frequencies are correlated on a bone-dry texture.

BOARD

SCENARIO: NON-VULNERABLE CONDENSED RANGE

Solver Model 9: Non-Vulnerable Condensed Range

Despite the inability to be perfectly condensed, the solver still checks with 100% frequency as we might expect.

It is interesting to note that the SB's overall range on this flop has a huge 78% equity share, which helps us to appreciate why high pot equity *alone* does not necessarily guarantee a high betting frequency.

SCENARIO: VULNERABLE CONDENSED RANGE

Solver Model 10: Vulnerable But Weak Condensed Range

In this model, we made the BB's air hands stronger so that they have a higher potential to suck out. This modification drops our equity down to 67% and the solver still recommends that we check our entire range.

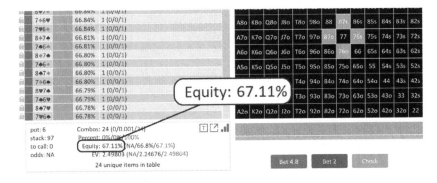

It turns out that it is fairly unlikely for purely condensed ranges to bet, even when they are a significant equity favorite. To some extent, this explains why we typically "check to the raiser" on the flop after calling an open raise or a 3-bet preflop.

Let us see if we can convince our solver to bet with its condensed range.

SCENARIO: WE HAVE A RELATIVELY VULNERABLE CONDENSED RANGE ON A DRY FLOP, BUT ARE A SIGNIFICANT EQUITY FAVORITE

Solver Model 11: Vulnerable But Strong Condensed Range

For this, we increased the number of air hands that villain has and kept all other parameters the same as in our previous model.

Our equity spikes to 76% and the solver recommends betting 27% of the time with a small bet sizing.

It seems that condensed ranges will bet for protection, but they need enough of an equity incentive before they spring to life.

Recall *Solver Model 6: Nutted Equity Distribution With Too Much Trash* from the previous chapter. We commented that the in-position player was advised to bet with their condensed range. The pot equity of the in-position player for that model was roughly 79% after facing the check.

SCENARIO: WE HAVE A RELATIVELY VULNERABLE CONDENSED RANGE ON A DRY FLOP BUT WE ALSO HAVE A NUMBER OF AIR COMBOS

Solver Model 12: Vulnerable But Strong Condensed Range With Air

This model is identical to the previous one, except we have added some air combos to the condensed range.

Interestingly, the solver now chooses to make use of the larger bet sizing despite the range being condensed.

We recall that GTO poker tries to continue with as many hands as mathematically possible in order to maximize the overall EV. In this case, using the larger sizing allows the solver to bet more of the air combos.

This is not to say that having those air combos is an advantage. The EV drops from 3.9bb to 3.4bb when we add the air combos into this second model. Our equity also drops from 76% to 64%. Despite this, our betting frequency actually increases from 27% to 65%.

We see again that betting frequency is not *purely* about equity. Having the air combos gives the range an incentive to bet more aggressively despite having less equity.

DID YOU KNOW?

A 5% range-versus-range equity advantage on the flop is typically considered very large. It is quite rare that one range has more than 55% equity against the other on the flop.

In the previous examples, we are getting more extreme range-versus-range equity differences because we are working with stripped-down game trees. These trees are less realistic overall, but easier for the human brain to follow every single combo and understand why it plays the way it does.

THE GEMS

- It is sometimes correct to work towards a condensed river range.

- Polarized/condensed range pairs get cleaner over the course of a hand, but are rarely perfect.

- Condensed ranges are only bet rarely, but if the range's equity is high enough they are bet for protection.

- Condensed ranges generally like to use small bet sizes when they bet, but may prefer larger sizes if they are air heavy.

FINAL ADVICE

We have made use of highly-simplified solver models in this chapter. Why not try running some more realistic solver models on your own and making predictions about how the solver will play?

....

BIG BLIND DEFENSE

Back in the early days of online poker, it was a well-known "fact" that players were supposed to defend a very tight range of holdings from the big blind when facing a button open raise.

The reasoning was fairly straightforward: it is hard to play poker out of position, so we can easily lose quite a chunk (or even all) of our stack when out of position postflop with a dominated holding.

It will probably sound crazy to a modern player, but looking down at KJo in the big blind when facing a button open could be quite an ordeal.

"We need to be super careful here. Villain is taking an aggressive action preflop and could easily have hands like AK, KQ, AJ, or even AA and KK. The safest option is surely just to fold."

It is possible that there were some good players back then who suspected that folding so much from the big blind might be incorrect. For the most part, however, many players just accepted that defending a tight range from the blinds was the way the game was supposed to be played.

After all, there was no decent way to verify the approach. But in today's era, we can use GTO solvers to create "solved" preflop ranges to investigate both antiquated and current approaches.

Preflop solves have the same limitations as any other type of solve, such as being dependent on the specified game tree. However, these solves give us a window into what correct preflop play looks like.

PREFLOP SOLVERS

Before we dive into some specific BB defense ranges, let us discuss a few of the technical details surrounding the creation of GTO preflop ranges.

Most solves that players are likely to run on a home computer are postflop solves. In such cases, the preflop ranges are manually given to the GTO solver as part of the game tree set-up.

The reason is straightforward: game trees with unknown preflop ranges are extremely large. To put some rough numbers on this, while a typical postflop solve might contain a tree size of around 8GB, a preflop solve might involve a tree size of more than 256GB.

The way solvers are built, it is necessary to have more RAM (a specific type of fast computer memory) than the size of the game tree being solved for. An average home computer will have anywhere between 4GB and 32GB of RAM, meaning they are perfectly adequate for postflop solves (in most cases) but do not even get close to the requirements for a decent preflop solve.

It is often necessary to rent a powerful cloud computer in order to run preflop solves. However, most players will not do this, and instead, choose to source a collection of solved preflop ranges from a trusted player or training site. They might then input these solved ranges into their home computer for the purposes of running postflop solves.

You can get all of our GTO preflop solves, and more, by getting the app at www.gtogems.com/app

GTO SOLVERS VERSUS NEURAL NETWORKS

DID YOU KNOW?

At Red Chip Poker, the Live Cash Game Preflop Solve took multiple months running 24/7 on a cloud server with a staggering 2TB of RAM. Simpler solves, like the 20bb MTT Preflop Solve, take closer to a week with 512GB of RAM running 24/7.

GTO solvers are not the only method for deriving game theory strategies.

Another type of GTO tool known as a "neural network" can be used to generate approximations of game theory play, including full preflop strategies.

So what is the difference between a GTO solver and a neural network?

Solver: This is essentially a calculator that iterates ranges against each other until a Nash equilibrium is reached.

Neural Network: This makes use of a machine learning algorithm. It plays trillions of hands against itself and slowly learns which lines generate the highest EV.

The most popular commercially-available neural network tool is *PokerSnowie*. Such tools are sometimes looked down upon by professional players because they are "not real solvers." In other words, they use an algorithm that is not based on finding a Nash equilibrium

However, neural networks have been used to great success in other competitive games such as *chess* and *Go*, where they have outpaced the best human players. We should not be too quick to discredit an approach that has proved so successful in the past for "solving" other complex games.

In addition, the end goal of a neural network is to maximize expected value just like a GTO solver does. We should therefore expect preflop ranges generated by a GTO solver to contain many similarities to ranges generated by a neural network. They are simply two different approaches to generating optimal preflop strategies.

We can likely reach the best understanding of GTO preflop strategies by considering both solvers and neural networks.

OPTIMAL BB RANGES

Here is a recommended BB defense range playing 6-max with 100bb effective stacks when facing a 2bb button open raise after the SB folds. It is produced using a neural network. (We will take a look at some GTO solver output in the next chapter).

AA	AKs	AQs	AJs	ATs	A9s	A8s	A7s	A6s	A5s	A4s	A3s	A2s
			80%	56%	4%							
AKo	KK	KQs	KJs	KTs	K9s	K8s	K7s	K6s	K5s	K4s	K3s	K2s
			95%	3%								
AQo	KQo	QQ	QJs	QTs	Q9s	Q8s	Q7s	Q6s	Q5s	Q4s	Q3s	Q2s
	17%			26%								
AJo	KJo	QJo	JJ	JTs	J9s	J8s	J7s	J6s	J5s	J4s	J3s	J2s
				94%								
ATo	KTo	QTo	JTo	TT	T9s	T8s	T7s	T6s	T5s	T4s	T3s	T2s
				13%								
A9o	K9o	Q9o	J9o	T9o	99	98s	97s	96s	95s	94s	93s	92s
A8o	K8o	Q8o	J8o	T8o	98o	88	87s	86s	85s	84s	83s	82s
						69%						
A7o	K7o	Q7o	J7o	T7o	97o	87o	77	76s	75s	74s	73s	72s
A6o	K6o	Q6o	J6o	T6o	96o	86o	76o	66	65s	64s	63s	62s
A5o	K5o	Q5o	J5o	T5o	95o	85o	75o	65o	55	54s	53s	52s
A4o	K4o	Q4o	J4o	T4o	94o	84o	74o	64o	54o	44	43s	42s
										63%		
A3o	K3o	Q3o	J3o	T3o	93o	83o	73o	63o	53o	43o	33	32s
A2o	K2o	Q2o	J2o	T2o	92o	82o	72o	62o	52o	42o	32o	22

The one thing that becomes apparent after looking at a selection of solved big blind defending ranges is that big blind defending ranges are very wide.

The idea of even deliberating for a moment whether KJo is a big blind call against a button open raise becomes somewhat laughable. The BB should even 3-bet with KJo at some frequency according to certain solvers.

Based on the above chart, we should even defend with any two suited cards and offsuit holdings as wide as K4o and 64o.

As a result, we have hands like J4s and 53s in our calling range. Overall, we are considering a 66% total defending range comprising a 11% 3-bet and a 55% calling range.

Of course, this is the most extreme example because the button may be opening for a larger sizing, in which case it is correct for the BB to fold more often preflop.

For example, here is the recommended defending range from the big blind against a button 2.5bb open.

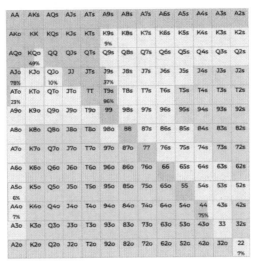

This is now a 44% total defending range comprising a 14% 3-bet and a 30% calling range.

Finally, here is the recommended defending strategy against a button 3bb open raise.

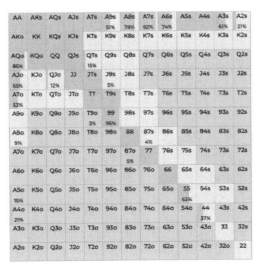

This is now a 31% total defending range comprising a 11% 3-bet and 20% calling range.

KEY LESSONS FROM THESE RANGES

LESSON 1: BB DEFENDING RANGES ARE WIDE

You may have been surprised by the number of hands we are supposed to defend from the big blind.

Take a moment and think about the defending ranges above. Do they match up with your current defending ranges in the big blind?

LESSON 2: SMALL CHANGES IN PREFLOP SIZING IMPACT THE SITUATION SIGNIFICANTLY

Notice how the overall defending frequencies change based on seemingly small changes in the size of the open raise.

	2BB	2.5BB	3BB
3-Bet Range	11%	14%	11%
Call Range	55%	30%	20%
Total Range	66%	44%	31%

LESSON 3: OUR OUTLOOK ON RE-RAISING DEPENDS ON THE SIZING

Did you notice the 3-bet frequencies in these ranges?

	2BB	2.5BB	3BB
3-Bet Range	11%	14%	11%

Notice that we 3-bet more aggressively against a 2.5bb open than we do against a min-raise.

We get an extremely good price on a call facing the min-raise and there is not a lot of direct incentive to take the pot down immediately.

Compare that against the 2.5bb open raise where we get a worse price on a call, but have a greater incentive to try and win our opponent's investment directly.

This is not to say that we will 3-bet progressively more often overall against larger sizings, since we are also required to defend an increasingly tighter range the larger the size of the open raise.

However, the distribution of our defending range does become more weighted towards re-raising the larger the size our opponent uses.

Note this table which shows the percentage of our defending range which is 3-bet depending on the size of our opponent's button open.

BTN OPEN SIZE	% OF DEFENDING RANGE THAT GETS 3-BET
2bb	16%
2.5bb	32%
3bb	36%
4bb	77%
5bb	51%
10bb	100%
25bb	100%

The pattern is fairly clear. Although we defend less often as their open sizings get bigger, a larger density of our overall defending range will be re-raises as opposed to calls. It simply is not *that* profitable to call against large raises preflop.

DEFENDING FROM OTHER POSITIONS

One of the key reasons why the big blind is defended with such a wide range is that we are closing the action against an open raise. Once we call from the big blind against a preflop open, we are guaranteed to see a flop for the price we have paid.

Another key reason is that we have already invested the mandatory 1bb blind payment, meaning that we get an effective discount on any call that we make.

The same factors do not hold true for other positions at the table, such as the button and small blind. GTO poker tools have confirmed that relatively little cold calling takes place from these positions.

For example, from the button facing a 2.5bb CO open raise, the neural network recommends cold calling 3% of the time and 3-betting 12% of the time. The GTO solver recommends cold calling 2% of the time and 3-betting 13% of the time. These results are by no means identical, but close enough for us to begin forming some sort of consensus on how best to play.

Both the GTO solver *and* the neural network recommend close to a 0% cold-calling range from the SB.

This is not a fair comparison though; the solver recommends a precisely 0% cold call since the option to cold call was removed from the game tree, as we will discuss further in the next chapter.

FACING PREFLOP 3-BETS

We can use what we have learned so far to extrapolate some basic rules regarding how to play in other preflop scenarios.

For example, imagine the common scenario where we open raise to 3bb from the button and face a 3-bet from the big blind.

How does our defending strategy differ based upon the 3-bet size?

We can guess immediately that we will defend less often facing larger 3-bets, but that our overall defending range will be weighted more towards 4-bets. Let us confirm this by looking at how our neural network defends against three different preflop 3-bet sizes.

3-BET SIZING	CALL	4-BET	% OF DEFENDS IS 4-BET
7bb	70%	2.4%	3%
10bb	47%	10%	18%
13bb	36%	11%	23%
30bb	2%	18%	90%

The last 3-bet sizing might not be incredibly realistic, but it helps to demonstrate that the distribution of 4-bets in the defending range will converge to 100%. There will become a point where flatting simply does not make any sense.

We can also see that the larger the 3-bet sizing, the less frequently we are supposed to defend. We defend 72% of the time versus a 7bb 3-bet, but only defend 20% of the time versus a 30bb 3-bet.

THE GEMS

- We should defend wider against smaller preflop raise sizings.

- A larger percentage of our defending range should be re-raises as our opponent's raise sizing increases.

- The big blind should do a large amount of cold-calling, because it closes the action and gets a 1bb discount when continuing preflop.

- We do not cold call very often from other positions at the table, especially the SB where we mostly 3-bet.

RAISING PREFLOP

Models of polarized river ranges were around long before the advent of solvers. It was understood that river betting ranges should be polarized when playing an optimal version of poker.

The extrapolation from this was to assume that ranges on the earlier streets of the game, including preflop, should also be polarized.

What we have seen so far in this book is that, while polarized ranges may start to form on the earlier betting rounds, they do not exist in their purest form until the river. This is especially true when thinking about preflop ranges.

PREFLOP POLARIZATION?

If we think about a polarized betting range on the river, it typically involves betting the absolute worst hands in our range along with the absolute best.

This is not true on any street before the river (aside from some very specific turn scenarios). For example, when we make a bet on the flop in NLHE, we do not generally do so with the absolute worst hands in our range. Although we do bet a selection of "bluffs," we typically select hands that have a measure of potential, perhaps through backdoor equity. GTO generally says that we should give up with the absolute worst hands in our range on every street before the river.

Similarly, although we may occasionally 3-bet preflop with some slightly more speculative holdings, we always fold with the worst hands in our range such as 32o or 73o. Even though optimal play involves "3-betting light," these 3-bet hands are carefully selected to be starting hands with a high degree of potential.

This is clearly very different from the type of polarization that occurs on the river in poker. Despite this, it is still common to hear the term "polarized" used to describe certain preflop strategies. Is this a proper use of terminology, or is it misleading? The goal is not to provide a specific answer here, but to give you something to consider as you continue through this chapter.

POLARIZED 3-BETTING?

The earlier we get in a hand of poker, the harder it is to spot any traces of polarization. For example, let us revisit the BB 3-bet range against a BTN 2.5bb open that we looked at in the previous chapter.

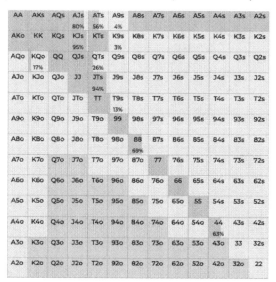

Ostensibly, this just looks like a linear range.

LINEAR

A linear range is simply a range containing the top x% of hands. The term *depolarized* is also sometimes used.

Raise-first-in ranges in poker are linear. It would not make sense to raise a selection of strong hands and weak hands while folding middling hands. We simply want to play the best possible starting hands preflop.

If any confusion occurs it is because we do not have a perfectly neat range; there is some mixing occurring.

We also note that some of the hands in the flatting range appear to be stronger than some of the hands in a 3-bet range! For example, K9s is in the flatting range, while T9s and J9s are mixed into the 3-bet range with some frequency.

We could certainly argue that the range is not perfectly linear/depolarized, but it is fairly hard to construct a case for the above range being deemed polarized. Besides, we could argue that T9s and J9s are actually better hands than KTs; not everything is about raw equity.

However, not all solved preflop ranges are as obviously depolarized as the above. For some of the larger 3-bet sizings, we see the solver becoming indifferent between 3-betting and cold calling with some of the weaker hands in the range.

For example, check out the following preflop range from a GTO solver. The scenario is identical except the game tree is given larger preflop 3-bet sizings. Red hands are 3-bets and blue hands are calls:

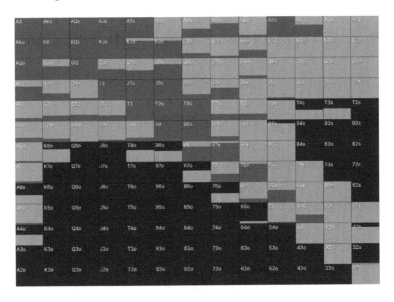

This range is a lot less easy to categorize.

We generally find clearer depolarization effects for smaller 3-bet sizings, but the above "breaking" effect occurs for larger 3-bet sizings. For very large sizings, we continue to see neat depolarization. In fact, the solver just flats a lot because it cannot 3-bet many hands profitably for such a large size.

It appears there is basically a sweet spot where it makes sense to 3-bet with more speculative hands.

If we 3-bet such holdings too small, we do not get sufficient equity denial. If we 3-bet too large, those speculative holdings are no longer strong enough to play at such a large 3-bet sizing and end up in the flatting range instead.

Should we then just try to 3-bet small so our 3-betting range is more linear? This does not provide us with an adequate solution. Besides, it seems logical that there should be some more speculative hands in the 3-bet range. We know that our eventual goal is to generate a polarized range by the river, and we need air hands in order to be able to do that. It is possible that the initial 3-bet ranges given to us by the neural network are *overly* linear.

Despite this, is it correct to refer to the above GTO solver range as *polarized*? Feel free to draw your own conclusion, but consider the following:

- All of the more speculative 3-bets are also mixed into the cold calling range with some frequency. There is no weak hand that only 3-bets but does not call.

- The weakest hands in the range are cold calls, not 3-bets.

- There is no obvious gap between strong and weak 3-bets, and there appears to be a relatively smooth distribution trending from stronger to weaker. For example, here is a heat map showing just the 3-bet range:

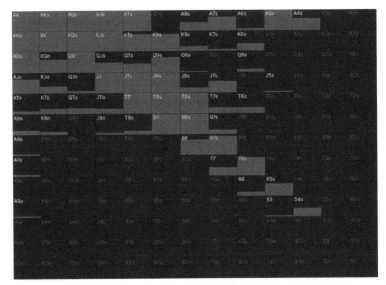

Regardless of whether we would view this range as "linear" or "polarized," it can never be "polarized" in the same way as a river betting range. Otherwise, we would see hands like 32o in the 3-betting range.

Besides, note the following "polarized" BB vs. BTN 3-bet range that was regularly used in the days before poker players had access to solvers.

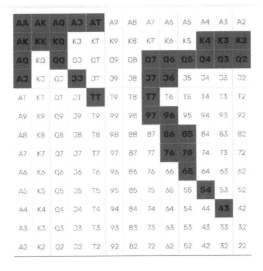

There is clearly a huge difference between this human-made polarized 3-bet range and the solver output from earlier. It would be strange to refer to *both* ranges as polarized.

We might instead use the phrase *depolarized range with mixing* to describe the construction of the solver range. Although there is some range protection with hands like A9s and AJo, the basic idea behind the solver range is to 3-bet almost all of our strong holdings. The more middling hands in our defending ranges will either be pure flats, or mixed between 3-bets and flats, depending on the exact game tree.

Another way of thinking about this mixing effect is that it represents the first characteristics of a polarized range beginning to form. We might use the invented term micro-polarization to explain scenarios where we see the first traces of polarization (these mixing effects) on the earlier betting rounds.

In the previous chapter, we saw that it is fairly ambitious to refer to flop ranges as condensed and polarized, but that we see the first characteristics of those ranges as they form across multiple streets.

The further back we go in terms of streets, the smaller the effects of the coming river polarization, but we may see the first traces of those ranges forming even preflop. By the time we reach the very first decision of the game tree (the raise first in, or RFI) ranges are now almost completely linear.

As an example of very clear polarization effects, check out the button's response when facing a BB 3-bet according to The GTO Ranges App:

AA	AK	AQ	AJ	AT	A9	A8	A7	A6	A5	A4	A3	A2
AK	KK	KQ	KJ	KT	K9	K8	K7	K6	K5	K4	K3	K2
AQ	KQ	QQ	QJ	QT	Q9	Q8	Q7	Q6	Q5	Q4	Q3	Q2
AJ	KJ	QJ	JJ	JT	J9	J8	J7	J6	J5	J4	J3	J2
AT	KT	QT	JT	TT	T9	T8	T7	T6	T5	T4	T3	T2
A9	K9	Q9	J9	T9	99	98	97	96	95	94	93	92
A8	K8	Q8	J8	T8	98	88	87	86	85	84	83	82
A7	K7	Q7	J7	T7	97	87	77	76	75	74	73	72
A6	K6	Q6	J6	T6	96	86	76	66	65	64	63	62
A5	K5	Q5	J5	T5	95	85	75	65	55	54	53	52
A4	K4	Q4	J4	T4	94	84	74	64	54	44	43	42
A3	K3	Q3	J3	T3	93	83	73	63	53	43	33	32
A2	K2	Q2	J2	T2	92	82	72	62	52	42	32	22

There seems to be a clearer middle portion to the range which is purely called: AQs, AJs, ATs A9s, and so on. We can definitely construct a slightly stronger argument for using the term "polarized" here.

Having said this, we also see that the "bluffs" are actually fairly high-equity hands, such as A3s and K7s. The weakest holdings in terms of equity that are defended (such as 54s) are purely flat calls. The absolute bottom of the range (such as J4s) is always folded and never defended.

It is fair to say that even if a raising range has much stronger components of polarization (or perhaps micro-polarization), it is still largely driven by equity at this early stage of a poker hand.

For comparison, here is the neural network range for the same scenario:

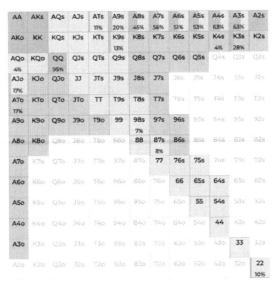

The similarities between the models are fairly impressive despite using two different techniques to arrive at a range.

True to form, the neural network is more linear than the solver range, and seemingly more interested in 4-betting Axs as opposed to mid-suited gappers.

Striking similarities include the flatting of A9s-AQs, the 4-betting of lower Axs, and the (almost) pure 4-bet strategy of QQ+.

Given this, quickly answer these three questions:

- Are these depolarized ranges with some mixing and range-protection?

- Are these depolarized ranges with the first micro-polarization effects beginning to appear?

- Are you convinced that these ranges should be referred to as polarized?

Ultimately, it might not matter too much which terminology we use to describe the range we see. But it is worth keeping in mind that the term polarization might be misleading in a preflop context. It carries the implication that we are 3-betting/4-betting a large proportion of the weakest hands in our continuing range, which is evidently not the case.

THE LIMITATIONS OF PREFLOP SOLVES

It is great to see how the neural network and solver show many similarities in almost every preflop spot. We can weigh the two methods up against each other and reach some sort of middle ground consensus.

However, we should remember that both types of GTO tools have limitations.

For example, we have discussed different 3-bet sizes, but which one is best? The neural network recommends a pot-sized 3-bet but is only given ½ pot, pot, and 2x pot to choose from. If the optimal sizing is slightly larger than the pot size, it cannot be revealed by using this particular tool.

Many GTO solvers have similar limitations and are only given a single 3-bet sizing to use. The solver is very capable of showing us how to play with that particular 3-bet sizing, but it gives us little indication of whether such a size is optimal in the first place.

We could try to give our solver a multitude of different 3-bet sizes to see which it chooses along with other insights, such as whether it is correct to mix our 3-betting range between two or more bet sizes. The problem is that this quickly becomes impractical since every extra decision option preflop significantly increases the size of the total tree.

It is common for tree builders to find ways to remove preflop options from the game tree, not to look for ways to *add* them. As an example, many GTO preflop solves involve a tree where the option to cold call is removed from every position apart from the big blind. This type of decision has many players incorrectly believing that the solver has chosen of its own accord to only 3-bet from certain positions, when in reality the solver could not cold call even if it "wanted to."

Similarly, we cannot conclude that a certain 3-bet sizing is best simply because the solver chose it. We need to look at the game tree first, since perhaps the solver did not even have a choice.

It is also worth remembering that it is typical to run GTO solvers only to a certain level of accuracy (otherwise the solve would take far too long). This might mean that certain weak hands appear in the 3-betting range as a result of inaccuracies in the solve, not because they should actually be there.

The same can be said regarding the neural network. Its strategy becomes more refined over time as it continues to play hands against itself, but perfect accuracy will not have been reached. Further, both the GTO solver and the neural network may make use of postflop trees which are non-optimal. Ironically, the solver would have to be able to make use of every single postflop sizing in order for us to determine whether the preflop sizings are optimal. Solvers just do not work like this, as the game tree would be unreasonably large.

The key takeaway is that *we should not blindly trust the output of a single solve or neural network*. Comparing multiple sets of preflop ranges and looking for an average result helps us to smooth over some of the inaccuracies.

THE GEMS

- We should RFI, 3-bet, 4-bet, and 5-bet with ranges driven by equity.

- Raising ranges contain mixing and range protection, but it might be misleading to refer to these ranges as "polarized."

- We can compare GTO solver and neural network preflop ranges to find a solid consensus.

- GTO preflop ranges are a great rough guide, but it is also crucial to understand the underlying game tree used to create them.

GEM #11

BLOCKERS DECIDE THE CLOSE SPOTS

It is quite common to hear "advanced" poker players justify the majority of their decisions by referencing blockers.

They will say things like *"I block villain's value range, so I will bluff here,"* or *"I block villain's bluffs here, so I will fold."*

Is this really the right way of thinking about poker hands?

Let us start by stepping back and defining what exactly is meant by the term "blockers."

BLOCKERS: CARD REMOVAL EFFECTS

> **BLOCKER**
>
> A card that we hold that makes it less likely (or even impossible) for our opponent to have certain types of hands. The fact that we can narrow our opponent's potential range by looking at our own two cards is a concept referred to as *card removal effects*.

As a simple example, if we hold the A♠, we know that our opponent cannot also hold it. If there are three spades on the board, we know that it is impossible that our opponent has the nut flush.

YOUR HAND   ## BOARD

Of course, our opponent may still have a spade flush of a different rank. But the overall likelihood of them holding a spade flush is decreased since we hold one of the spades. We can correctly say that we are *blocking* some of our opponent's possible flushes.

THE IMPACT OF BLOCKERS ON STRATEGY

Let us return to one of our earlier models: *Solver Model 3: Multiple Sizings Demo.*

As a quick recap, the aggressor was given a range that included nutted value hands, but also a selection of slightly weaker non-nut value hands. The purpose of the model was to see which one of the two sizings the solver preferred for the different types of hand.

BOARD

AGGRESSOR (OOP)													DEFENDER (IP)												
AA	AK	AQ	AJ	AT	A9	A8	A7	A6	A5	A4	A3	A2	AA	AK	AQ	AJ	AT	A9	A8	A7	A6	A5	A4	A3	A2
AK	KK	KQ	KJ	KT	K9	K8	K7	K6	K5	K4	K3	K2	AK	KK	KQ	KJ	KT	K9	K8	K7	K6	K5	K4	K3	K2
AQ	KQ	QQ	QJ	QT	Q9	Q8	Q7	Q6	Q5	Q4	Q3	Q2	AQ	KQ	QQ	QJ	QT	Q9	Q8	Q7	Q6	Q5	Q4	Q3	Q2
AJ	KJ	QJ	JJ	JT	J9	J8	J7	J6	J5	J4	J3	J2	AJ	KJ	QJ	JJ	JT	J9	J8	J7	J6	J5	J4	J3	J2
AT	KT	QT	JT	TT	T9	T8	T7	T6	T5	T4	T3	T2	AT	KT	QT	JT	TT	T9	T8	T7	T6	T5	T4	T3	T2
A9	K9	Q9	J9	T9	99	98	97	96	95	94	93	92	A9	K9	Q9	J9	T9	99	98	97	96	95	94	93	92
A8	K8	Q8	J8	T8	98	88	87	86	85	84	83	82	A8	K8	Q8	J8	T8	98	88	87	86	85	84	83	82
A7	K7	Q7	J7	T7	97	87	77	76	75	74	73	72	A7	K7	Q7	J7	T7	97	87	77	76	75	74	73	72
A6	K6	Q6	J6	T6	96	86	76	66	65	64	63	62	A6	K6	Q6	J6	T6	96	86	76	66	65	64	63	62
A5	K5	Q5	J5	T5	95	85	75	65	55	54	53	52	A5	K5	Q5	J5	T5	95	85	75	65	55	54	53	52
A4	K4	Q4	J4	T4	94	84	74	64	54	44	43	42	A4	K4	Q4	J4	T4	94	84	74	64	54	44	43	42
A3	K3	Q3	J3	T3	93	83	73	63	53	43	33	32	A3	K3	Q3	J3	T3	93	83	73	63	53	43	33	32
A2	K2	Q2	J2	T2	92	82	72	62	52	42	32	22	A2	K2	Q2	J2	T2	92	82	72	62	52	42	32	22

AA,77,33-22,AKs,A9s-A8s,A6s,A2s,98s,
86s-85s,65s,AKo,A9o,A2o,98o,96o,86o-85o,65o

AQs-AJs,A7s,J7s,T7s,97s,87s,
AQo-AJo,A7o,J7o,T7o,97o,87o

For the most part, the nutted value hands chose the larger bet sizing, while the weaker value hands chose the smaller bet sizing.

There are a couple of notable exceptions though:

- Pocket Aces (nut full house), which can never be beaten by any hand the defender holds, is solidly in the small bet sizing range.

- A2s and A2o (full houses) are mixed between the small and large sizings, despite also being unbeatable.

We could argue that the solver needs to protect its small bet-sizing range with some premiums. However, it could just as easily achieve this by mixing all of the strong holdings into the small bet sizing with an equal proportion. So why has the solver specifically singled out the AA and A2 combos?

Let us take a look at the defender's calling range against the larger bet sizing for some clues.

AA	AK	AQ	AJ	AT	A9	A8	A7	A6	A5	A4	A3	A2
AK	KK	KQ	KJ	KT	K9	K8	K7	K6	K5	K4	K3	K2
AQ	KQ	QQ	QJ	QT	Q9	Q8	Q7	Q6	Q5	Q4	Q3	Q2
AJ	KJ	QJ	JJ	JT	J9	J8	J7	J6	J5	J4	J3	J2
AT	KT	QT	JT	TT	T9	T8	T7	T6	T5	T4	T3	T2
A9	K9	Q9	J9	T9	99	98	97	96	95	94	93	92
A8	K8	Q8	J8	T8	98	88	87	86	85	84	83	82
A7	K7	Q7	J7	T7	97	87	77	76	75	74	73	72
A6	K6	Q6	J6	T6	96	86	76	66	65	64	63	62
A5	K5	Q5	J5	T5	95	85	75	65	55	54	53	52
A4	K4	Q4	J4	T4	94	84	74	64	54	44	43	42
A3	K3	Q3	J3	T3	93	83	73	63	53	43	33	32
A2	K2	Q2	J2	T2	92	82	72	62	52	42	32	22

Note that the defender is almost exclusively calling with Ax holdings against the large bet sizing. This results in a defending frequency of around 40%, which is enough to prevent the aggressor's bluffs from being profitable.

Bearing in mind that the aggressor wants a call as frequently as possible here, there is a small problem. Due to blocker effects, it is less likely the defender has Ax, and more likely that they instead have one of the 7x holdings when the aggressor is trying to value bet their AA and A2 combos.

This means the defender will actually be folding more than 60% of the time, because the defender has part of their folding range *more often than we would normally expect.*

Let us assume for a moment that the Ax hands in the defender's range are pure calls (just to keep things simple). We can calculate and compare how many combos the defender has without blocking effects, as opposed to when the aggressor holds either AA or A2 specifically.

BOARD

DEFENDER'S HAND	NORMAL COMBOS	COMBOS VS. A2	COMBOS VS. AA
AQ	12	8	4
AJ	12	8	4
A7	9	6	3
Total Combos:	33	22	11
~Folding Frequency:	59%	69%	81%

Holding A2, we will generate a 69% folding frequency, which is not great when trying to extract value. The solver calculates that the EV of value betting large and betting small is the same.

However, with 81% equity when trying to extract value with AA, the solver calculates that it is more profitable to always bet small rather than trying to bet large. Such card removal effects would be great if we were trying to bluff, but they significantly lower our EV when we are trying to extract value with the nuts against such a specific calling range.

Although value betting AA in the smaller bet-sizing range is still far from ideal in terms of card removal effects, a number of the defender's 7x holdings are now forced to call (since the defender needs to call wider against smaller bet sizings).

The solver calculates that this is higher EV for the aggressor overall, and thus uses the AA combos purely in the smaller bet sizing range.

PRINCIPLES FOR USING BLOCKERS

There are more gems embedded in this model. Note the following two key lessons:

1. WHEN DEFENDING, WE PREFER BLUFF-CATCHERS THAT BLOCK OUR OPPONENT'S VALUE-BETTING RANGE, BUT DO NOT BLOCK THEIR BLUFFING RANGE.

Remember how the defender was calling all Ax hands and folding all 7x hands? The defender was not doing this arbitrarily, simply because Ax hands are stronger than 7x hands. Ax and 7x have effectively the same hand strength in this scenario, because both of them beat the aggressor's bluffs, but lose to their value hands.

If there was no card removal effect at work, the solver would likely just bluff-catch all of these hands with the same frequency. We saw examples of this in the perfect polarization solver models.

In this case, it is more profitable for the solver to bluff-catch Ax holdings due to card removal effects. We know that the aggressor's value range consists entirely of hands that hold at least one Ace. When the defender holds an Ace, it means the aggressor has less Aces and is showing up with range that is slightly more weighted towards bluffs.

Conversely, it is ideal if the defender's bluff-catchers do not block the bluff combos that are used by the aggressor. Such bluff-catchers would shift the aggressor's bluff-to-value ratio further towards value combos. For example, if the aggressor were bluffing mostly with 98o (which is not true in this case), the defender would prefer to bluffcatch with T7 rather than with 98 and 87.

2. WHEN BLUFFING, WE PREFER BLUFFS THAT BLOCK OUR OPPONENT'S CALLING RANGE, BUT DON'T BLOCK THEIR FOLDING RANGE.

The solver selects the 56 combos as the aggressor's bluffing range for the large bet sizing. Currently, the defender is folding all combos over 87, 97, T7 and J7 in favor of defending the Ax combos.

Ideally, the aggressor's bluff combos should not block any of those cards, since it will reduce the number of folding combos the defender has (and thus, the defender's overall folding frequency).

In this instance, a combo like 98 would be a particularly bad bluff for the aggressor, since it removes some of the 87 and 97 combos from the defender's range (lowering their folding frequency). It makes sense that the solver chooses 65o, since it is the only combo that maximizes the width of the defender's folding range.

Where possible, it is also advantageous if bluffs can block the defender's calling range.

In this instance, it would involve holding one of the side cards from the hands with which the defender calls. If the aggressor has it in their own range, something like Q5o would be an ideal bluff candidate here, since it blocks the AQ combos in the defender's calling range while not blocking any of the defender's folding range.

For the smaller bet-sizing range, we see that the aggressor bluffs both 56 and 96 combos with some frequency. So why the addition of 96 to the bluffing range? If we look at the defender's range against the smaller bet sizing, we see them now calling a number of 97 combos. As such, the 96o combos now block some of the defender's wider calling range.

Why did the defender specifically start widening their range with 97 combos before other 7x bluff-catchers? Because 97 blocks the A9 combos that are being used as part of the aggressor's thin-value range.

SO IT IS CORRECT TO THINK ABOUT BLOCKERS?

Realistically, the answer is probably: no. Or at least *not to the extent* that modern players prioritize blockers in their strategic model.

It was fairly straightforward to understand how the blocker effects were working above, because we had such a simple model. A real-world situation is far more complex. Note first that we would require almost perfect vision regarding our opponent's range to even begin to compute which blocker effects that we have.

At the same time, our opponent is trying to adjust their own use of blockers to prevent us from being able to get an advantage through using blockers. Sometimes the most obvious use of blockers actually invites counter-exploitation. Thus, GTO models can result in some fairly counter-intuitive combo selections after a Nash equilibrium is reached.

This means it is arguably close to impossible (for a human) to work out which blockers are favorable in practice; and that is already assuming we know our opponent's range perfectly (which we probably do not in real time).

The other big elephant in the room is that the use of blockers to make a decision assumes the spot is extremely close. This is mostly only true if our opponent is also very good. If our opponent is instead making errors, such as folding way too often on the river, we should generally just bluff all of our air combos. Not only would thinking about blocker effects be a waste of energy in that situation, but it would actually lower our win-rate if we made the decision to not bluff based on a certain blocker.

The next time we hear an "advanced" poker player basing their decisions around blocker effects, it is worth remembering that card removal effects are only a tiny detail in a huge picture. They should not be the fundamental concept that drives our decisions, unless we are playing against a perfect GTO robot.

THE GEMS

- Blockers are used for hand selection in very close spots.

- Many hands end up being close in a perfect GTO world. Against inferior opponents, many spots are not that close and blockers are not important in finding the best line.

- Theoretically, when bluffing, we prefer to block our opponent's calling range, but not their folding range.

- When choosing bluff-catchers as the defender, we prefer to block our opponent's value-betting range, but not their bluffing range.

GTO SIMPLIFICATIONS

We have seen that game theory optimal poker is complex; far too complex to be implemented accurately by a human player.

As we might imagine, this does relatively little to stop humans from wanting and trying to play GTO poker.

At some point, disseminating down from high-stakes circles (as a lot of good poker information usually does), came the idea that it is possible to play a simplified version of GTO that is not significantly inferior to a full GTO strategy in terms of expected value.

Earlier in this book, we already touched on examples of this type of simplification. For example, the idea that we can eliminate preflop cold-calling ranges at certain positions at the table is a type of GTO simplification.

SIMPLIFICATION: 3-BET ONLY PREFLOP

Technically, perfect GTO poker involves cold calling from every position at the table. Even cold calls in the small blind are recommended by solvers (although it does depend somewhat on the set-up of the postflop game tree).

That said, we generally find that our overall expected value is not heavily impacted if we simply remove all of our preflop cold calling decisions, apart from those in the big blind.

This is not to say that our EV will not be impacted at all, but the loss in EV is often surprisingly small. The advantage is that we end up with a simplified game tree. As human players, we only need to remember one range (our 3-bet range) and we do not need to worry about playing any parts of the game tree where we are the cold caller from non-BB positions (since we are removing cold calling).

We have now *significantly* reduced the amount of work required to learn the various facets of an operable game plan. We might still be using GTO techniques to derive our strategy, but we are deliberately assuming the game tree is simpler than it actually is.

This is just one example of a common GTO simplification. We can use the same logic to simplify other areas of the game as well.

SIMPLIFICATION: ONE BET SIZING

Earlier in the book, we discussed how using multiple bet sizings is mandatory for playing perfect GTO poker.

This has not changed, but it might be worth exploring how much EV those multiple bet sizings are actually worth in certain situations.

For example, let us return to *Solver Model 4: A More Realistic Multi-Street Solve*. We used this model to generate a realistic equity distribution graph for river play, but we never deeply explored the model.

The solver model represents a situation where the small blind raises first-in preflop and faces a cold call from the big blind. For c-betting options, the solver is given a range of four different sizes to choose from.

It is rare that we would give a solver four different bet-sizing options at any given decision point, but this tree originally had the specific purpose of analyzing GTO flop bet sizings. The exact details of the tree are not too important, although it is designed to make use of realistic starting ranges on a K72 rainbow board.

①	Bet 5.1	0.33%	②
	Bet 3.96	0.03%	②
	Bet 3	22.8%	②
	Bet 1.98	35.8%	②
	Check	41.1%	②

The solver does not seem particularly interested in the larger two sizings here, but it does use the two smallest sizings quite frequently. (Note there is 6bb in the pot so the smaller sizes are ⅓-pot and ½-pot, respectively).

The solver also tells us that the EV of the entire decision, including all bets and checks, is 2.84bb.

Since the solver uses the one third sizing most frequently, let us recreate the tree and force the solver to always either bet ⅓-pot or check.

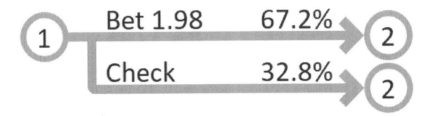

The solver actually bets *more* frequently overall when it does not have access to the larger sizings. Amazingly, the EV of the overall decision remains at exactly 2.84bb according to the solver.

You will have to trust us that this does not normally happen! In many cases, the EV drops *slightly*, but not enough to make any significant impact. For example, the EV dropping to 2.80bb (instead of 2.84bb) might be a fairly typical result here.

Our flop strategy is now a lot easier to execute since we do not have to think about distributing our range across four different bet sizes. However, we are still left with a fairly complex mix of bets and checks.

What happens if we force the solver to instead always bet, and remove checking entirely?

SIMPLIFICATION: ALWAYS BETTING

If we remove the solver option to check (forcing it to always bet the flop for ⅓-pot) our EV drops to 2.74bb. This is not an especially big drop given that we can now implement the strategy perfectly by firing a

⅓-pot continuation bet with our entire range.

Hypothetically, we can make 0.1bb more on average if we play a more complex strategy, but it will be very difficult to execute with any real accuracy due to the complex mixing.

What often happens in practice is that we *lower* our EV even further with the more complex strategy, since we make quite a number of mistakes in trying to execute it.

The conclusion is that, for a human, a slightly *less accurate* but *more consistent* strategy will usually yield better results in the long run.

FINDING LOGICAL SIMPLIFICATIONS

The simplifications we just made were based upon the existing strategy of the solver.

We selected the ⅓-pot bet sizing because it was the sizing most commonly employed by the solver initially. If the solver had clearly preferred a different bet size, we would have attempted to simplify by using that bet size instead.

We then forced the solver to bet with its entire range because it was already betting 67% of the time anyway. If the solver had been betting less than 50% of the time, we would have likely simplified by asking the solver to check 100% of the time instead.

In that spirit, what happens if we take the above model and force the solver to check with its entire range rather than bet? This would be a seemingly less logical solution in general. Interestingly, despite this, the EV actually increases to 2.79bb (from 2.74bb). This shows the value of sometimes exploring beyond the most obvious simplification.

It seems that the solver is not heavily affected by having its flop options simplified, since it is able to compensate for this by making perfect GTO adjustments on the later streets.

Oversimplifying turn and river decisions becomes much riskier. This is not to say that we cannot simplify, but certain options can heavily impact our win-rate.

For example, let us revisit our first model *Solver Model 1: Perfect Polarization Model*. The initial EV of the aggressor's strategy is 71bb and the solver likes to bet frequently due to the polarized range. What happens if we force the solver to check? Our EV drops significantly to 47bb.

Admittedly, that might not be the most logical simplification. What happens if we force the solver to always bet? The aggressor's bluff-to-value ratio will now be unbalanced towards bluffs, meaning that the defender has a profitable call with all of their bluff-catchers. This might seem the lesser of two evils, but our equity drops even further to 41bb! It is actually better for the aggressor to never bet their polarized range at all, rather than to bet with a range that is too far weighted towards bluffs.

Regardless, neither of these simplifications are acceptable. We are simply losing too much in EV relative to a more accurate GTO strategy.

This does not mean that we cannot simplify by reducing the number of available bet sizes. For example, we might get away with having a single bet size on the turn and two on the river (or something similar). Forcing the solver to always check or always bet on the later streets might not be a smart option.

Although GTO simplifications may make some of the earlier streets easy to play, we have no choice but to embrace a measure of complexity at some point in the game tree. Our overall EV will still be defined by how well we deal with the complex decisions on later streets.

GTO simplification techniques can be helpful in that they allow us to *reduce* the amount of complexity we need to face overall, and *delay* that complexity until later into a poker hand on average.

A FINAL REMINDER

The world of GTO poker is rich and awesome. While understanding GTO will make us stronger poker players, it does not mean that GTO strategies will make the most money in every game (or even most games).

Although a "simplified" GTO strategy may appear to perform almost as well as a full GTO strategy, both approaches might be giving up significant profits relative to an exploitative strategy.

Throughout this book, we have seen examples of how we might adapt when our opponent is deviating from GTO principles in formulating their own strategy. In most cases, our default assumption should be that our opponent will not be capable of finding the relevant counter-adjustment if we try to exploit them.

We would therefore only make use of GTO simplification techniques against good opposition when there is no clear exploitative opportunity (at that specific decision point). However, we will look to branch out to an exploitative strategy later on in the hand if exploitative opportunities present themselves.

Exploitative play makes the most money, but it is a solid understanding of GTO poker that allows us to recognize and take advantage of those exploitative opportunities in the first place.

THE GEMS

- It is possible to simplify a GTO approach without significant loss of EV.

- It *is* necessary to use a solver to verify the quality of potential GTO simplifications.

- We are very flexible with early street simplifications, but need to be much more cautious when thinking about turn and river situations.

- Use GTO when incentivized, but play exploitatively where possible.

CONCLUSION

Instead of writing a boring conclusion that very few people will bother to read, it seemed more valuable to put The Gems from each chapter here. If you need a quick refresher on any of the big takeaways from this book, this will serve as a helpful resource.

CHAPTER 1 GEMS

- While a complete GTO solution may exist for complex games like NLHE and PLO, it will be impossible for a human to accurately implement.

- You do not need to play perfect GTO poker in order to win at poker.

- Exploiting your opponents' mistakes will be more profitable than rigidly sticking to a GTO approach.

- Simple games, like RPS, offer a clear visualization for using versus deviating from a GTO solution.

- A player who wins more hands does not necessarily win the overall game, because different amounts of chips are wagered on each hand.

CHAPTER 2 GEMS

- We should bet a mixture of bluffs and value hands while on the river. (This is known as a polarized range.)

- The larger our river bet sizing, the more frequently we should be bluffing.

- Value bets should account for the larger portion of our range, even when using large sizes.

- The GTO bluffing frequency for the aggressor is the same as the pot odds percentage offered to the defender.

CHAPTER 3 GEMS

- There is a perfect middle ground between how often we fold and how often we continue against our opponent's bets.

- The larger our opponent's bet sizing, the more often we should fold.

- We can calculate the break-even point of our opponent's bluff by looking at the percentage of the total pot they are investing.

- We should defend at a frequency that makes our opponent's bluffs 0EV (assuming the perfect polarization model).

CHAPTER 4 GEMS

- Always play every hand in our range at its maximum EV.

- Mixed strategies are a requirement for GTO play.

- Mixed strategies are only used when the EV of two (or more) lines is the same.

- We often need to protect weak ranges with some stronger holdings.

- Mixed strategies are less important against weak opponents.

- There may be a limit to how far we push exploits against advanced opposition.

CHAPTER 5 GEMS

- It is impossible to play GTO poker without the use of multiple bet sizes.

- The sole objective of any poker player should be to exploit their opponent as hard as possible.

- Without multiple sizings, some of our hands will not be able to maximize their EV by playing at their preferred sizing.

- Strong holdings often bet large, but they also need to be used in smaller bet sizing ranges for range protection.

- Bluffs should appear in all bet-sizing ranges using the appropriate bluff-to-value ratio.

CHAPTER 6 GEMS

- It is impossible to know the correct GTO strategy by only considering the raw pot equity of our range.

- The range that has the most pot equity is not necessarily the most profitable to play.

- Consider the equity distribution of both players' ranges.

- Some aspects of a range are more valuable than raw equity, such as having the polarized range and/or having the nutted equity distribution.

CHAPTER 7 GEMS

- A nutted equity distribution usually means large bet sizes.

- An advantage deeper in the range usually means smaller sizes.

- We bet at a higher frequency if our range contains many hands that have the correct characteristics for betting.

- Hands bet either to build a pot or for equity denial.

- Pot equity is more likely to be correlated with betting frequency for deeper range advantages.

CHAPTER 8 GEMS

- It is sometimes correct to work towards a condensed river range.

- Polarized/condensed range pairs get cleaner over the course of a hand, but are rarely perfect.

- Condensed ranges are only bet rarely, but if the range's equity is high enough they are bet for protection.

- Condensed ranges generally like to use small bet sizes when they bet, but may prefer larger sizes if they are air heavy.

CHAPTER 9 GEMS

- We should defend wider against smaller preflop raise sizings.

- A larger percentage of our defending range should be re-raises as our opponent's raise sizing increases.

- The big blind should do a large amount of cold-calling, because it closes the action and gets a 1bb discount when continuing preflop.

- We do not cold call very often from other positions at the table, especially the SB where we mostly 3-bet.

CHAPTER 10 GEMS

- We should RFI, 3-bet, 4-bet, and 5-bet with ranges driven by equity.

- Raising ranges contain mixing and range protection, but it might be misleading to refer to these ranges as "polarized."

- We can compare GTO solver and neural network preflop ranges to find a solid consensus.

- GTO preflop ranges are a great rough guide, but it is also crucial to understand the underlying game tree used to create them.

CHAPTER 11 GEMS

- Blockers are used for hand selection in very close spots.

- Many hands end up being close in a perfect GTO world. Against inferior opponents, many spots are not that close and blockers are not important in finding the best line.

- Theoretically, when bluffing, we prefer to block our opponent's calling range, but not their folding range.

- When choosing bluff-catchers as the defender, we prefer to block our opponent's value-betting range, but not their bluffing range.

CHAPTER 12 GEMS

- It is possible to simplify a GTO approach without significant loss of EV.

- It is necessary to use a solver to verify the quality of potential GTO simplifications.

- We are very flexible with early street simplifications but need to be much more cautious when thinking about turn and river situations.

- Use GTO when incentivized, but play exploitatively where possible.

We hope that you have enjoyed this book and received a sizable amount of value from it. If you are looking for even more strategy, both exploitative and GTO, please be sure to join us at www.redchippoker.com today.

In the meantime, good luck and happy grinding!

BONUS OFFERS

(AND MORE)

THE PREFLOP & MATH WORKBOOK

The optimal way to improve your technical skills is to practice them the right way between sessions. This workbook bridges the gap between theory and practice by teaching you the key concepts & formulas and helping you internalize them through focused exercises.

Complete a few pages per day and train your brain to correctly calculate pot odds, implied odds, ranges, break-even percentages, and even EV. Then pair those skills together with preflop-specific plays like isolating, 3-betting, squeezing, 4-betting, and going all-in.

This workbook includes 1,500+ questions, a complete answer key, both cash game and tournament examples, plus a companion course so you know exactly how to do each section.

Save $10 when you use the code **GEMS** at checkout.

WWW.GTOGEMS.COM/PREFLOP

THE POSTFLOP WORKBOOK

Postflop is complex. With so many different possibilities between flop textures, runouts, and available lines, it sometimes seems impossible to know where to start. This is where **The Postflop Workbook** comes in.

This workbook arms you with the technical knowledge required to find real profit during sessions. By leveraging modern learning methods, you will understand board textures, how often ranges hit vs. miss, where to find auto-profit, and how to craft lines for value hands and bluffs alike.

Grab your copy today with 1,700+ questions, a complete answer key, both cash game and tournament examples, along with a training course so you know exactly how to do each section.

Save $10 when you use the code **GEMS** at checkout.

WWW.GTOGEMS.COM/POSTFLOP

PRO PASS

The PRO Membership from Red Chip Poker has everything you need to take your strategy to the next level. PRO Members get access to the entire PRO video library, CORE, The GTO Ranges App, and more.

Here are just a few of the courses you can get started with now:

- **The Bet-Sizing Course.** Get a complete sizing foundation, examples that bridge the theory and application, and an understanding of how key variables come into play.

- **The MTT Course.** This multi-part series guides you through tournament play at the theoretical and applicable levels. If you are a cash-game player looking to take some shots at tournaments, watch this course first!

- **Player Pool Analysis.** Learn how to exploit quantifiable mistakes your player pool makes leveraging real data.

As a bonus, you can **get your first 3 months of PRO for just $99**. Study the right material at your own pace, and if you ever get stuck, simply let us know on Discord and we will craft a study plan for you.

WWW.GTOGEMS.COM/PASS

GLOSSARY

Balance. A byproduct of playing every hand in our range at maximum EV against a perfect GTO opponent.

Blocker. A card that we hold that makes it less likely (or even impossible) for our opponent to have certain types of hands.

Bluff. A bet with a very weak hand hoping to get our opponent to fold.

Bluff-Catcher. A hand that can only win if our opponent is bluffing. In the context of a GTO discussion, a bluff-catcher will also be at least strong enough to beat all of our opponent's bluffs.

Bluff-To-Value Ratio. This relative number of value hands and bluffs in a given betting (or raising) range.

Break-Even Point. How often a bluff needs to work in order to be profitable in the long run. If a bluff works more frequently than the break-even point, it will be profitable. If the bluff works less often than the break-even point, it will be a losing bet.

Combinations (Combos). How many ways a type of hand can be made. For example, there are six possible ways to be dealt a given pocket pair preflop, so there are six combos of each pocket pair.

Condensed Range. A range that contains primarily middling hands that lose to the value hands against a polarized range, but beat the bluffs. Technically, polarized and condensed ranges should always appear in pairs, as it is impossible to have one without the other.

Equity. Also known as *pot equity*, this term refers to how often a hand or range can expect to win at showdown if there is no further betting action. It is often thought of as a player's rightful share of the current pot, based on the strength of their hand or range.

Equity Denial. Betting to capitalize on the fact that our opponent will fold out their equity share. This is typically done with weak and mid-strength hands, despite the fact that these combos may already be the best hand with some frequency.

Equity Distribution. How equity is distributed across a range in comparison to another range.

Expected Value (EV). A measurement of how profitable a poker decision is over the long run, measured in either big blinds or a currency amount.

Exploitative. A strategy that is not considered game theory optimal, but is instead designed to take advantage of the mistakes that our opponent is making. (A "mistake" is any deviation our opponent makes from perfect GTO play.)

Game Theory Optimal (GTO). Game theory is a branch of mathematics that deals with calculating strategies for competitive situations (such as playing poker and other strategy games). If a poker decision is GTO, it means it is mathematically the best possible decision when facing a perfect opponent.

Game Tree. A game tree is a diagram containing all the possible game states for a certain game. In poker, the game tree represents all the possible actions, boards, hands, and bet sizes that are possible across the entire game.

GTO Solver. This is essentially a calculator that iterates ranges against each other until a Nash equilibrium is reached. The postflop solver that Red Chip Poker recommends is called **GTO+** given its cost and ease of use, and is available for purchase with an entire training course here: www.gtogems.com/solver

Linear. A linear range is a range containing the top x% of hands. Linear ranges include the best possible starting hands and then "the next-best" starting hands (with all included hands being in the upper left-hand corner of a range matrix. The term *depolarized* is also sometimes used.

Mixed Strategy. A mixed strategy is where a certain poker hand is required to take differing actions at certain frequencies. For example, when facing a bet, GTO poker might require a hand to call 70% of the time and raise 30% of the time. This is the opposite of a *pure strategy*.

Nash Equilibrium. The game state where no player can increase their win-rate by deviating. In poker terms, a Nash equilibrium is achieved when two players are playing perfect GTO poker against each other.

Neural Network. Hardware employing a machine learning algorithm. In the context of poker, it plays trillions of hands against itself and slowly learns which lines generate the highest EV.

Nutted Equity Distribution. A range is said to have the nutted equity distribution when it contains hands that are so strong that the other range can never beat them (at least not without additional cards being dealt).

Polarized. A polarized range is comprised exclusively of strong value hands and bluffs, and no hand strengths in between.

Pot Equity. How often a hand or range can expect to win at showdown if there is no further betting action. It is often thought of as a player's rightful share of the current pot based on the strength of their hand or range.

Pot Odds. The "price" a player gets on a call when facing a bet (or raise). This can be expressed as either a ratio or as a percentage of the total pot invested.

Pure Strategy. A pure strategy is one in which a hand takes a certain action with 100% frequency (for example, it always calls). This is the opposite of a mixed strategy.

Range. Short for "a range of possible holdings," this term refers to all of the hands with which a player might take a specific action. For an expanded definition and examples, go here: www.gtogems.com/ranges

Range Advantage. The range that is more favorable (or more profitable) than another is said to have range advantage, regardless of the ranges' overall pot equity.

Range Protection. The act of including some stronger holdings in checking and small bet-sizing ranges so that these ranges can defend themselves.

Simplification. The act of removing options (bet sizings, actions, etc.) from a game tree in an attempt to make implementation easier, while sacrificing the least amount of EV compared to more complex solutions.

Value Bet. A bet with a strong hand (i.e. a value hand) that is designed to get called by worse holdings.

CONNECT WITH US

Follow us on your favorite social media platform to get more poker strategy and discussion.

RED CHIP POKER

Facebook	redchip.poker/fb
Instagram	redchip.poker/insta
Twitter	redchip.poker/twitter
YouTube	redchip.poker/youtube

JAMES "SPLITSUIT" SWEENEY

Facebook	splitsuit.com/fb
Instagram	splitsuit.com/insta
Twitter	splitsuit.com/twitter
YouTube	splitsuit.com/youtube

DISCORD

Join our free Discord server today. Share hands, ask questions, and jump in the conversation with thousands of players who love poker as much as you do.

WWW.GTOGEMS.COM/DISCORD

Made in United States
Orlando, FL
29 July 2022

20309295R00072